Facets of Ayn Rand

Frank O'Connor and Ayn Rand
1964

Facets of Ayn Rand

Memoirs by Mary Ann Sures and Charles Sures

AYN RAND
INSTITUTE PRESS

First printing November 2001
10 9 8 7 6 5 4 3 2 1

http://www.aynrand.org/

ISBN: 0-9625336-5-3

Production by Ronen Nakash
Cover design by David Layne
Cover photograph courtesy of the Estate of Ayn Rand

Table of Contents

The Ayn Rand Archives
Oral History Program

The Ayn Rand Archives Oral History Program was established in 1996 by the Ayn Rand Institute (ARI) to gather and preserve knowledge of Ayn Rand's business, creative, and personal life. To date, Scott McConnell, oral historian, has conducted 169 interviews (about 300 hours) with Miss Rand's family, friends, and associates. The interviews reveal considerable new information about Ayn Rand's life, from her early years in Russia, to Hollywood, to her many years in New York City. Selected interview transcripts are currently being prepared for publication.

Facets of Ayn Rand is based on 48 hours of interviews with Mary Ann and Charles Sures, prepared and conducted by Mr. McConnell from September 1998 to January 1999. It is the first publishing project of the Oral History Program.

Introduction by Leonard Peikoff

Mary Ann and Charles Sures were longtime personal friends of Ayn Rand – Mary Ann for twenty-eight years, Charles for almost twenty. Their recollections in this delightful memoir make vividly real the Ayn Rand they knew so well.

Their book offers plentiful examples of Ayn Rand's mind, and intellectual generosity, in action, and also captures many lesser-known aspects of this unique woman. In these pages, we see Ayn Rand the celebrity, the loving wife, the legal client (of Charles), the employer (of Mary Ann). We are with her in her study (including the day she wrote the last page of *Atlas Shrugged*), at stamp shows, at the opera, on a New York City transit bus, in the White House. We discover new examples of her favorite and least favorite things in clothes, perfume, parties, music. We relish again her sense of humor, her capacity for indignant anger, her benevolence.

The Sures understand and admire the passion for values from which Ayn Rand's anger stemmed. In Mary Ann's words, she was someone "who always speaks out, unequivocally, against irrationality and injustice, and who not only denounces evil, but *who defends the good.* She was mankind's intellectual guardian, a soldier in the battle of ideas. Her banner was always flying high. When she died, someone made the following comment: 'now anger has gone out of the world.' And I thought, it's true, and it's the world's loss, and mine."

As to Ayn Rand's response to the good, Mary Ann describes some eloquent scenes, such as: "I had heard that when [Ayn's] ship reached the pier [from Russia], tears ran down her face as she looked up to the skyline of New York. I asked what those tears were for. Frank answered: 'They were tears of splendor.' And Ayn nodded in agreement."

The unique quality of these memoirs is not only the new content they reveal, but also the perfect balance they achieve among ideas, emotions, and actions, including where appropriate specific dialogue and physical, perceptual details. The result has almost the impact of fiction, specifically of Romantic characterization. From the book one gains not a mélange of random memories, abstract ideas, and disconnected concretes, but rather the experience of an actual larger-than-life person.

The person in this book is the same person I myself knew for so long; reading these pages is almost like having Ayn Rand in the room again. The result on me is partly sadness that the irreplaceable is gone, but mostly exhilaration that she once was real.

Admirers of Ayn Rand owe a debt of gratitude to the Sures for their dedicated work in putting this compelling material on record. They finished the manuscript just before Charles died last December. He spent considerable time during his last weeks and even days in editing and polishing his parts of the book. Knowing how near he was to death, he still said to Mary Ann: "It's one of the most important things we have ever done. We have to make it just right." This is the kind of heroism before which one stands hushed, in farewell salute.

Ayn Rand and her husband would have grieved at Charles's death. I know this because I know the values they shared, and what friends the four of them were. The Sures were among the few people in Ayn Rand's life who were intellectually honest all the way down: they accepted her philosophy, they lived by it, they remained loyal to it and to her throughout her life and theirs. Thus the special feeling Ayn Rand communicated whenever she spoke of them.

Those who want to know more about the author of *The Fountainhead* and *Atlas Shrugged* now have a new opportunity to do so – thanks to the loving memories of two lovely people, Mary Ann and Charles Sures.

Irvine, California
March 2001

—

Our Approach to These Interviews

ARI: What is your purpose in doing these interviews?

MARY ANN: We want to preserve our recollections of Ayn Rand and our evaluation of her. Few people knew her for as long as we did – I for twenty-eight years and Charles for almost twenty. She was an extraordinary thinker and person, and we knew her in both capacities. In the years to come, people will be asking the same question they ask about her today: what was Ayn Rand like as a person, in her private life? We can answer that question.

ARI: Is part of your reason to pay a debt of gratitude to her?

CHARLES: That's part of it. What we, and many, many others, owe to her is incalculable. But, in addition to that, we have read things about her that give a distorted picture of what she was like. We want to correct the record. It should be said here that we are not referring to Leonard Peikoff's essay, "My Thirty Years with Ayn Rand: An Intellectual Memoir."[1] That is a brilliant analysis of her thinking methods, and it captures the spirit of Ayn Rand the philosopher and person.

ARI: Why do you think people are so interested in knowing about Ayn Rand the person?

MARY ANN: I think it's akin to falling in love with someone. When you do, everything about that person becomes important to you. From his basic outlook on life to small details. For the

---

[1] Leonard Peikoff, Epilogue, *The Voice of Reason* by Ayn Rand, New American Library, 1988

same reason, but not with the same intensity, people who have come to value Ayn Rand through her writings want to know more about her. That's a legitimate interest, motivated by the desire to give reality to the person they admire but know only as an abstraction – as "philosopher" and "fiction writer."

CHARLES: I should add that this is *not* what motivates today's tabloid mentalities. They look for flaws and shortcomings, for weaknesses. They debunk greatness, to get at what they claim is the "real" person. This is a miserable outlook on man and life; it reflects the medieval view that man is imperfect by nature.

MARY ANN: We are concerned with the woman who defined the philosophy of Objectivism, who let us enter the bright, shining worlds she created in *The Fountainhead* and *Atlas Shrugged*, who straightened our intellectual spines and made it possible for us to lift our heads and look up and out, and to step forward into great distances with certainty and conviction. That's the woman we are going to talk about. *That* is the "real" Ayn Rand.

CHARLES: Ayn Rand was a rare, one-of-a-kind, multi-faceted jewel. We want to hold some of those facets up to the light.

Chapter I

Ayn Rand and Mary Ann Sures

Ayn Rand in Her New York City Apartment
1952

MEETING AYN RAND

ARI: Where, when, and how did you meet Ayn Rand?

MARY ANN: I met her in New York, sometime in the fall of 1954. The occasion was an oral examination on her philosophy.

ARI: In those years, where did you have the opportunity to study her philosophy?

MARY ANN: Privately, with Leonard Peikoff, who was then a graduate student in philosophy at New York University (NYU). Here's the background, briefly. At the time, I was an instructor teaching art history at New York University, Washington Square College, while pursuing a Master's Degree in art history at NYU's Institute of Fine Arts. An acquaintance I met in graduate school, Joan Mitchell,[1] gave me a paperback copy of *The Fountainhead*. We had been discussing art history as a career choice, and I told her that I had been criticized for studying art when there were starving people in the world whom I should help. I didn't agree with that attitude, but I didn't have convincing arguments against it. Joan said that I would find the answers in that novel. I did, and I loved the book.

Joan, who had met Ayn Rand some years earlier, introduced me to Nathaniel Blumenthal[2] and his wife, Barbara, who were close friends and admirers of Ayn and her writings. They were

---

[1] Joan Mitchell later married Allan Blumenthal and is known professionally as Joan Mitchell Blumenthal.

[2] We called him Nathan. He later changed his last name to Branden.

graduate students at NYU, he in psychology, she in philosophy. Nathan wanted to meet people interested in and in agreement with the ideas expressed in *The Fountainhead.* I also met Leonard Peikoff, another admirer of Ayn Rand. Since Leonard wanted to teach philosophy, Nathan suggested that it would be good experience for Leonard to give private lectures on Ayn Rand's philosophy to a few people, including me. This was Leonard's first course on Objectivism, although it wasn't yet called "Objectivism." He gave some of the lectures in Joan's apartment. It was an informal set up.

ARI: What topics did he cover?

MARY ANN: He explained what philosophy is, and then focused on metaphysics, epistemology, and ethics. He explained the Law of Identity, causality, sense perception and reason, altruism, man's life as the standard, the benevolent universe concept.

Leonard Peikoff

ARI: Had you studied philosophy before this?

MARY ANN: Very little. I had had a bad experience in an introductory college course in philosophy. The professor, a Platonist, made philosophy obscure and unrelated to living. Leonard's lectures were the opposite: he made the ideas clear, and he showed the relevance of philosophy to life. I typed up my notes and went over them with Leonard to make sure I understood everything. He was a dedicated teacher, even then. Incidentally, I kept those notes for more than 30 years, along with my first paperback copy of *The Fountainhead* – until the book and the notes crumbled and fell apart.

When the lectures were finished, it was decided that there would be an exam and that it would be oral and held one evening at the home of Ayn Rand. I learned later that she suggested it.

ARI: Didn't you feel intimidated about the prospect of meeting her under those conditions?

MARY ANN: No. I had read and reread *The Fountainhead* and I had studied my notes from Leonard's lectures, so I felt prepared. That's one reason I didn't go there with butterflies. But the main reason has to do with my perspective and context then. When you or I say "Ayn Rand" today, we think of a genius, an intellectual giant: the creator of the philosophy of Objectivism, the author of *Atlas Shrugged, The Fountainhead,* and *We the Living,* the writer of an impressively long list of brilliant articles, essays, and lectures. But, when I met her in 1954, the context was different. She was still writing *Atlas Shrugged*; the essays and lectures were yet to come; her classic *Introduction to Objectivist Epistemology* was twelve years way; *We the Living,* which I had not read, was out of print. Yes, she *was* then a genius, an intellectual giant. Only I didn't know it. I had read only *The Fountainhead,* and I wanted to learn more. So, when I went to the exam, I was eager, naive, and ignorant, but not nervous. I had no idea of how extraordinary a person she was. Of course, by the time the evening was over, I did.

ARI: What do you remember of that evening of more than forty years ago?

MARY ANN: I'll say first that in one's lifetime, there can be events of such significance that they are never entirely forgotten. Meeting Ayn Rand is in that category, and my memory of aspects of the evening is still fresh. Also, in those days, I kept a diary of sorts; I recorded my impressions of that night.

I was the first one to arrive; Frank [O'Connor][3] admitted me to the apartment and, after saying that Ayn would be out shortly, left me alone in the living room. It was a long room lit by lamplight falling on glass-topped end tables and comfortable, clean-lined furniture. I walked over to the window; the drapes were open, and there were no buildings nearby to interfere with the view toward downtown Manhattan. For a few minutes, I stood at the window. Then I heard a sound behind me, and a voice said, "Hello." I turned around, and there was Ayn Rand.

I had imagined someone quite different, someone tall, blonde and slender, like a fifty-year-old Dominique,[4] someone reserved in manner, even a little bit aloof. But she wasn't like that at all. She was shorter than I expected,[5] and her hair was brunette.

---

[3] Ayn Rand and Frank O'Connor were married in 1929.

[4] Dominique Francon, in *The Fountainhead*

[5] Ayn Rand was about five feet tall.

There was nothing aloof in her manner. When I turned, she had the nicest, friendliest smile. She was standing in the middle of the room, so I walked over to her and introduced myself. We shook hands, and she commented on my name being Russian with the feminine ending. I was Mary Ann Rukavina then. I remember only two things about our first conversation: I told her that I had thoroughly enjoyed *The Fountainhead*. She thanked me and asked if there were parts or characters that I especially liked. I answered, "The boy on the bicycle."[6] She smiled broadly. That was how we met. It was very simple, very natural.

She was wearing a navy blue outfit – a skirt and jacket, with a blue and white polka dot blouse. I learned later that it was an outfit designed by Adrian.[7] She wore high heels. She had a simple hair style, with a touch of the dramatic – a short, straight bob that angled across her forehead. Her eyes were deep brown, large and luminous, wide open. They were always like that; she never seemed to squint. Soon, others came and the examination started.

ARI: Who was running it? Who was there?

MARY ANN: Leonard was in charge – he was the professor. Joan and I were the only students. Frank, Barbara, and Nathan were there, as observers, along with Ayn.

ARI: What do you remember about the exam?

MARY ANN: I don't remember all the questions, but there were some on the Law of Identity, and on causality. Joan and I took turns and added to each other's answers. We did well.

I remember one episode very well, because Ayn was speaking directly to me. I was having a problem with an issue in metaphysics, which was a new field for me. Ayn could tell from one of my answers that I didn't understand the distinction between "attribute" and "entity." She sat on an oversized couch that was covered in plaid tweed. I can see her there now! There was a rectangular chrome-and-glass-topped coffee table in front of her. Using the table as an example, she explained the distinction to me. She explained that the "length" of the glass top was an at-

---

6 The beginning sequence of Part Four
7 Gilbert Adrian, a famous Hollywood designer, and his wife, actress Janet Gaynor, were friends and neighbors of the O'Connors in Chatsworth, California.

tribute, which couldn't exist apart from the "entity" glass top; and she discussed the height, width, and smoothness of the glass, explaining that they were also attributes.

A few times, she stopped her explanation to ask me if it was clear to me. She said she wanted to make sure I understood one point before going on to the next one. Without realizing it, each time I grasped a point, I smiled. And she asked me why I was smiling, and I answered that I was happy to understand it. And then she smiled in response.

That night, I learned two things about her that were true of her all the years I knew her: one, she took ideas seriously, and two, it mattered to her that her listener understood her. Her knowledge was vast, her context was broad, but she could explain complex ideas in a manner that could be understood by someone without that knowledge and context. And when you grasped a point, she was pleased and she showed it.

Some years later, we were discussing one of her favorite television series, *Perry Mason*, and she commented on how much she liked Raymond Burr's facial expression in the introductory credits. He is in a courtroom, holding a legal document and looking thoughtful. Then he begins to smile, slowly and knowingly. Ayn said that he looked as if he had made a mental connection, had understood something, as if a light bulb had been turned on in his mind. For her, observing a mind following an argument and making mental connections was like seeing a light bulb go on in the mind of her listener – and this was a source of great pleasure for her. I responded to this aspect of her that night, and I valued it throughout our friendship. She never changed.

ARI: How would you describe her general manner?

MARY ANN: She was intense about the importance of ideas, and she was intensely focused when explaining them. But what came across was this: to deal with ideas, to communicate them, to understand them – this is the most natural thing in the world for people to do. She spoke from the premise that philosophy is everyone's business because it affects everyone's life; it is not some dry, esoteric subject taught by disillusioned professors. By her tone of voice, her way of looking directly at you when she was speaking, she let you know that she was explaining an idea to *you, to you personally,* and that it was vital that you understood it.

ARI: What else impressed you?

MARY ANN: Something she conveyed that was unusual. Here was a person who really cared if an idea was true and right. She was not a disinterested philosopher. Truth *mattered* to her, not just intellectually, but emotionally. When she discussed ideas, there was an urgency, an exhilaration in her manner. She was concerned with truth, the whole truth, and nothing but the truth. That was a rare attitude.

ARI: Rare, in what respect?

MARY ANN: Other people might be concerned with impressing you with the extent of their knowledge, or with their status in your eyes, or with being a celebrity, or with any number of things irrelevant to the subject under discussion. Not Ayn Rand, not that night, or ever. Nothing got in the way, nothing interfered with her focus on what was true, no matter what the issue was. She made it clear that we were there for one reason: to understand issues in philosophy and learn what was true and what was false.

But there was something else about Ayn Rand that was different from anyone I had ever met before. I felt myself responding to this "something," but I didn't know what it was. It wasn't until after a few more meetings with her that I could name it.

ARI: What was that?

MARY ANN: *She had certainty.* This is what really attracted me emotionally to her that night. She was the first person I had ever met who projected it – she projected that what she knew was true, and that she was sure of it.

What she was that night was the way she always was: she never doubted herself and her capacity to understand. It's not that she had an encyclopedic mind that knew everything – although she knew more about things than most people did. The point is that she didn't live in a state of chronic doubt. She didn't constantly question the rightness of her ideas. She didn't hesitate and flounder. She spoke with conviction. What she knew, she knew. This was a strong element in her personality.

ARI: What did it mean to you, personally?

MARY ANN: She was like fresh water, in unlimited supply, made available to a person dying of thirst. You see, I did not grow up in an atmosphere of religious mysticism. The problem for me was skepticism, although I didn't know it at the time. I grew up in an intellectual environment that almost everyone grows up in, that communicates one thing: you can't really be sure of anything. Which is another way of saying that you can't trust your mind to know reality. Of course, as a child, you could be sure of the multiplication tables in arithmetic, or the correct spelling of a word – things you memorize. But when it came to ideas, to reaching conclusions, to understanding people and judging them – the attitude was, "who can say for sure what is true or false, what is right or wrong?"

The problem plagued me throughout childhood and into high school and college. Skepticism in teaching methods led to endless research and reading, to constantly consulting "authorities" who disagreed with one another, to collecting fact upon fact – but never reaching firm conclusions; everything had to be tentative, on principle. Skepticism was everywhere, and some people seemed to resent it if you wanted certainty. Once, in graduate school, I called a work of sculpture "ugly," and the professor hit the ceiling. How can you be sure, he said, of what is beautiful or what is ugly?

And then I met Ayn Rand. Not only was *she* certain, but she conveyed that *you*, too, could be certain of your knowledge, that you shouldn't accept anything less.

When I got to know her better, I commented on her certainty. And she said, very simply, that if by observation and reason she concluded something was true, then there was no reason for her to doubt it. New evidence might cause her to revise her thinking, but until and unless such new evidence was available, she was firm about the rightness of her conclusions.

ARI: Is there anything else you recall from that first meeting?

MARY ANN: I was impressed with her manner of speaking – she spoke in complete sentences; she didn't grope for words or examples. There was an economy in the way she used words; she spoke right to the point. She smoked throughout the evening, using a long cigarette holder, and occasionally she used it as a baton to emphasize a point. She had a pronounced Russian accent, but she spoke as someone who is completely at home with the English language. That shouldn't have surprised me, not after having read *The Fountainhead* and having seen firsthand her command of the language. But the combination of her accent and the ease with which she spoke English was startling. Later, I learned that she had worked very hard on mastering English. She had been conscientious about studying all the shades of meaning of any word and making her definitions precise.

ARI: How would you describe the general atmosphere of that evening?

MARY ANN: There was a prevailing sense of good will, which was created in large part by Ayn. I've talked about her serious attitude, but there was a charming aspect to her, too. Before she commented on my confusion about "attribute" and "entity," she turned to Leonard and asked him if he wanted to clarify it for me, or if he minded if she did. I was impressed by this – she was respectfully deferring to the professor. He said that she could do it, that he wanted to hear her on the subject. Then, when she concluded her explanation, she turned to him and said, smiling, "Well, how did I do?" – in the manner of a student seeking the professor's approval. It was delightful. I left that evening knowing that I had never met anyone like her. Now, almost fifty years later, I can still say the same thing.

AYN RAND'S CERTAINTY

ARI: Mary Ann, getting back to your positive response to her certainty. Did anyone ever accuse you of being attracted to her because you wanted an authority figure in your life?

MARY ANN: Yes, I used to hear that frequently – but I haven't heard it for many years. It didn't take me long to learn that although it was said as a criticism of me, the real target was her philosophy and her certainty that her philosophy was right.

ARI: Could you elaborate on this point?

MARY ANN: Some critics have tried to turn her certainty into a desire on her part to be an authority in the bad sense, and they accuse her of being dogmatic, of demanding unquestioning agreement and blind loyalty. They have tried, but none successfully, to make her into the leader of a cult, and followers of her philosophy into cultists who accept without thinking everything she says. This is a most unjust accusation; it's really perverse. *Unquestioning agreement is precisely what Ayn Rand did not want.* She wanted you to think and act independently, not to accept conclusions because she said so, but because you reached them by using your mind in an independent and firsthand manner. She was adamant about it: your conclusions should result from *your* observations of reality and *your* thinking, not hers. Now, she could help you along in that process, and, as we all know, she did. But she never wanted you to substitute her mind for yours.

ARI: Charles, you must have some thoughts on this issue. Why do you think some critics claim the opposite to be the case?

CHARLES: What it comes down to is that they resent her for her ideas. They resent certainty and what it comes from – from holding reason as an absolute, from basing one's knowledge and conclusions exclusively on observation and thinking conceptually, from holding a consistent, integrated philosophy. She often stressed that last point – that Objectivism is an *integrated* philosophy, that it cannot be accepted piecemeal, that one cannot take an option on principles of Objectivism and apply them only when and if it is convenient – that is, when they don't clash with irrational desires and deceptive behavior. Some people attempted to do that. And whenever she saw evidence of it, she did not let it go by. She always named the issue, always called a spade a spade. She made it clear that you can't have your cake and eat it, too. You cannot say you hold reason as an absolute and then indulge in petty evasions, or go back on your word, or breach contracts, or tell lies to get a value you don't deserve, or say that everything is a matter of opinion, that everything is relative. When she saw someone doing this, she didn't let them get away with it. She named what they were doing. She always brought reason and reality back into the picture.

WORKING FOR AYN RAND

ARI: Mary Ann, you were one of Ayn Rand's typists of *Atlas Shrugged*. Let's talk about that experience. How did it come about?

MARY ANN: In the fall of 1956, Ayn was nearing the end of the writing, and needed a typist and proofreader. I had just finished a teaching assignment at NYU and was looking for employment that would leave me some free time to do graduate work. By that time, she knew me well enough to know that she could trust me not to divulge the content of the novel to anyone.

ARI: How long did the job last? And what did you do?

MARY ANN: It lasted until the spring of 1957, when she turned the completed manuscript in to Random House. In the beginning, it wasn't full-time work. Some days there wasn't much to type, but as the weeks progressed, the workload increased. On some days, I was there from morning to evening.

When I started, the work consisted of typing and proofreading the newly written pages of the novel. That was a memorable experience. I had the pleasure, and the privilege, of reading the last part of the novel in her handwriting – hot off the press, so to speak.

In the fall of 1956, she was writing the closing chapters of Part III. She was also editing the entire novel from page one, all of which had been typed by previous secretaries. I retyped the extensively edited pages that were difficult to read. On the pages that had very little editing, I made the changes in pencil on the carbon copies. In the beginning, we always discussed which pages needed retyping, and which pages could get by with pencil changes. After a while, she left it up to me. She wanted to present a manuscript that could be read easily. One of the sections she especially wanted to submit in clean pages was Galt's speech. I did considerable retyping of it.

ARI: Let's talk about those months.

MARY ANN: Having had Ayn Rand as a mentor and friend for twenty-eight years was itself a matchless experience. But that period, the fall of '56 and spring of '57, has a unique place in my thoughts and memories, because it was during this period that I really got to know Ayn and Frank, and they got to know me, on a personal basis. We developed a closer relationship. Until then, I had seen them mainly in the company of others, or if I was alone with her, the discussion was usually about an aspect of philosophy. Now, I was alone with them almost on a daily basis, and the context was different. There were just the four of us in the apartment – Ayn, Frank, Frisco the cat, and me.

ARI: Frisco the cat?

MARY ANN: Oh, yes. He was a member of the O'Connor household – he was a much loved, beautiful animal. And he played his part in the finishing of *Atlas Shrugged*, as you will see.

ARI: Where were they living at the time?

MARY ANN: In the fall of 1956, Ayn and Frank lived at 36 East 36th Street, Apt. 5-A. Across the street from the apartment house was the splendid Morgan Library. Around the corner was B. Altman, a department store which has since closed; Frank enjoyed shopping there. Across from B. Altman was a hamburger shop, Tailor Made, from which the O'Connors ordered.

ARI: Could you describe their apartment?

MARY ANN: Their apartment was a one bedroom with den; it was not very spacious. You entered into a short hallway which opened into a larger entrance foyer. A black-lacquered dining room table was kept in the foyer, pushed up against a mirrored wall. I worked at the dining room table. Beyond the foyer was the living room, long and rectangular, with windows at one end. To the left of the foyer, there was a short hallway leading to the bathroom, linen closet, and the kitchen. Around the corner, there was another short hallway leading to her study and to their bedroom.

It was very compact. The foyer, where I worked, was very close to her study – not more than 10 or 12 steps. She kept the door to her study open, and, when necessary, we could talk back and forth.

ARI: She didn't close the door for privacy?

MARY ANN: Only when she had a personal phone call. Otherwise it was always open.

ARI: What was her study like?

MARY ANN: It was very small, and very simple. Actually, it was quite bare. There was only one window, and her desk was placed right in front of it. She didn't have an inspiring view, just windows of an apartment house across the way. To the left of her desk, along an adjoining wall, there were book shelves. On one of the bottom shelves, she kept the typed manuscript of *Atlas Shrugged* in boxes that had contained typewriter paper. The hand written pages she was working on were kept in manila folders on the desk; she did her writing on a blue-green blotter. Opposite the desk were filing cabinets, on which there was a telephone and a pencil sharpener.

ARI: No decoration, no personal touches in the room?

MARY ANN: Two personal touches. On the wall to the right of the desk, there were three photographs of Frank which were publicity stills from the Hollywood days, taken when he was a young man. He was strikingly handsome. Hanging next to these photographs was a print of an industrial site. So she had Frank and modern industry nearby, both what she would call "top values." And, the desk was a gift from Frank; he had had it made for her. So that's a personal touch, too.

The floor was parquet, not carpeted. She sat in a

straight-backed, wooden chair that had a thin cushion covered in blue-green material. When she got up, she scraped the chair against the wooden floor, and I could easily hear it. The floor in the hallway was tiled, and I could hear her brisk footsteps. And Frank's, too, which were longer and more leisurely. And she could hear my typing – which didn't seem to disturb her.

ARI: Let's talk about a typical workday. How did it start?

MARY ANN: Starting time was 9:00 a.m., unless we had agreed to a different schedule. Frank usually answered the door. He always told me what Ayn was doing – "Ayn is at her desk," or "Ayn is having coffee in the bedroom," or, very seldom, "Ayn is still sleeping." If Ayn was not working yet, he would tell me to help myself to the freshly made coffee, and join them in the bedroom for a morning visit.

ARI: What did you talk about?

MARY ANN: Movies or television shows we had seen, or current events, sometimes art. They were not lengthy discussions.

One morning, early on, I rang the doorbell and I heard her quick steps approaching the door, and then her deep voice: "Hallo?" she said. "It's Mary Ann," I answered. Then she opened the door a crack and asked me to excuse her because she wasn't dressed. That's how I learned that Ayn Rand often worked in a nightgown. The one she wore was made of a soft material, like brushed jersey. It was pale aqua, and it fell to the floor in long, regular folds, like a Greek column. The sleeves were long and full, and the neckline was a wide V decorated with rhinestones. It was quite glamorous. She had slippers in aqua leather, to match. She once jokingly assured me that she had other nightgowns, but this one was her favorite, and it was warm and heavy enough to wear without a robe.

When she was dressed, which was most of the time, she usually wore a navy wool skirt and a simple, short-sleeved silk blouse – in navy or dark green. And her favorite pair of high-heeled red leather sandals.

The first time I saw her in the nightgown, she explained why she wasn't dressed: if, when she woke up, she felt refreshed and eager to start writing, she didn't want to lose the momentum. So, she would quickly splash water on her face, brush her teeth, run a comb through her hair, get a cup of coffee, and get right to work.

ARI: What was she like when she was writing?

MARY ANN: She was very disciplined. She seldom left her desk. If she had a problem with the writing – if she had what she called the "squirms" – she solved the problem at her desk; she didn't get up and pace around the apartment, or wait for inspiration, or turn on the radio or television. She wasn't writing every minute. Once I heard a flapping sound coming from the study – she was playing solitaire. She might read the newspaper. At times, I entered the study to find her sitting with her elbows on the desk and resting her chin on her hands, looking out the window, smoking, thinking.

One morning when I arrived, she was still in bed. I started my work, and soon I heard her call out: "Oh, Frank. I'm falling asleep. Oh no, I can't!" A few minutes later I heard her slippers slapping on the tiles. She washed her face, took a cup of coffee, and went to work. Later that morning, she explained that she had been up very late the night before, and had had little sleep. She had a deadline to meet with Random House, and she was determined to meet it – exhausted or not.

ARI: Did she ever play music while she worked?

MARY ANN: Only once, in my experience. When she was writing the last chapter of the novel. One afternoon she put a record on the stereo, which was in the living room, and asked me to replay it when it stopped. It was the last movement of Rachmaninoff's *Second Piano Concerto*.

ARI: Do you know what scene or dialogue she was writing then?

MARY ANN: No, I don't, and I was curious, too. But I didn't think it was my business to ask. And, had I asked, she would have answered – or explained why the question was too personal.

ARI: This brings me to the question: what kind of a boss was

Ayn Rand?

MARY ANN: She was, in a word, a lovely boss, very easy to work for. She never issued terse orders, or showed impatience, or stood over my shoulder. She was not your stereotypical temperamental genius. There was a graciousness in her manner – there was always "please" and "thank you" when she had a request. But she wasn't chatty; there was seldom any small talk before I started to work, if she was already at her desk. We agreed on the day's work and I got right to it.

This raises what I call the spiritual atmosphere of the household. In a few words, it was sheer, unadulterated, never-ending good will – an atmosphere created by both Ayn and Frank. Here were two unpretentious and considerate people. In that home, there were no meta-messages or hidden agendas or speaking between the lines – there was always complete candor. And no tension hanging in the air. It was, truly, a benevolent universe.

When there wasn't a full day's work for me, she apologized. I didn't mind; I used to float to work, eager to get there. Once, I told her that I liked coming over because it was a sane and friendly place, and she said, "Oh?" in her characteristic way, and nodded and said, "Well, yes it is, you're right." And she added that I was free to come over and bring work of my own on days when I wasn't scheduled to work for her.

ARI: And did you?

MARY ANN: Only a few times, because I thought it was an intrusion. But, she was sincere about it; they treated me like one of the family. I should have taken her at her word, because she meant everything she said.

She was a woman without moods. Or, if she were in a mood, she knew it. She would say so and offer a reason.

ARI: Such as?

MARY ANN: If her work had been interrupted for some reason – like attending to some business matters or going to the dentist. That always got her down, and she knew it.

In the morning when I entered the study to get my work, I

tapped lightly on the open door so I wouldn't startle her. There were only a few times when she didn't acknowledge me with a smile and a hello.

She was patient. It took me a while to get used to her handwriting. So, in the beginning, on the days I typed up the newly written pages, I read them over first. And if I had any questions, she wanted me to interrupt her. I tried to keep interruptions to a minimum. In all the months I worked for her, she only got angry with me once.

ARI: About what?

MARY ANN: She didn't like typewritten pages with just a few lines. She thought they interrupted the flow of the story for the reader at Random House. Short pages resulted from deletions or additions to the typed manuscript, and were often unavoidable. However, when we were nearing the end of the editing and re-typing, one of her changes resulted in adding some lines to the manuscript; I ended up with a page that had only three or four lines. To make it a complete page would have required re-typing all the pages up to the end of that section, and there just wasn't time. Well, when she saw it she got angry. She reminded me, in very stern tones, of our agreement to avoid short pages. She explained again her reasons for not wanting to trouble the reader. I thought her point was valid. But, I have to add here that I wasn't feeling very sympathetic toward that reader, who had the pleasure of reading the novel in large sections, in one sitting – while I had had to wait for Saturday nights to read single chapters and then spend the week wondering what was going to happen next! So, when she finished, I just said, "Ayn, it's *Atlas Shrugged* we're talking about." She just looked at me, and her expression changed; she said, simply, "You're right." I think we were both a little on edge, working against a deadline.

ARI: What were the working conditions, physically?

MARY ANN: I worked on an old manual typewriter, with a cotton ribbon that wound around spools, and the ribbon and the keys stuck occasionally. I heard once that she had brought a typewriter with her from Soviet Russia. I don't know if this was that typewriter, but it could have been. It was like an old tank, and just as noisy! I typed an original and several carbon copies, and I made corrections with a typewriter eraser. This was long before the days of word processing!

In the beginning, I was quite slow and didn't think I was earning my day's wages, so I suggested that she pay me by the page. It would have been to her financial advantage, but she insisted on paying me by the hour at the going rate. She said she knew I would pick up speed after I got used to the typewriter. And she insisted that I keep records of minutes, and if I stayed 10 minutes over an hour, she insisted on paying me for a quarter of an hour.

She didn't expect me to do personal errands for her. I did shop at a nearby stationer's for typing supplies, and that was part of the job. The one time I volunteered to do a personal errand, there was a long discussion.

ARI: What was that?

MARY ANN: A few times a week, in the early afternoon, she would interrupt her work to call in the grocery order. The O'Connors bought their groceries from Verde's, a small, specialty grocer on Third Avenue, near 36th Street, which was a few blocks from their apartment. She had to get the order in by a certain time so that it could be delivered late in the afternoon. One day, she missed the deadline. Verde's delivery boy was gone for the day, and Frank wasn't home, so I volunteered to pick up the groceries.

ARI: What happened?

MARY ANN: First she said it was out of the question, that she couldn't ask me to do that, that doing personal errands was not part of my job, and so on. She referred to types she had known in Hollywood and of which she disapproved – executives who always expected personal favors and errands. And I explained that the situation was an exception, that it was necessary, and that I didn't mind the walk. I don't remember the entire exchange, but I managed to convince her. But she insisted on paying me for the time and having me stay for dinner. She definitely didn't exploit her employee. I was always treated with respect; she always held my context. They both did.

ARI: Were there any house rules?

MARY ANN: I remember three. First, to make sure that all cigarettes one smoked were put out in the ashtrays, especially in the ashtray on her desk. She was very strict about that. I often saw her carefully stubbing out a cigarette in the desk ashtray. If she thought there might be something still burning, she carried the ashtray into the kitchen. Another rule was the way I destroyed manuscript pages of *Atlas*.

ARI: Are you saying that you actually destroyed pages of that novel?

MARY ANN: Yes. If a typewritten page had extensive editing and had to be retyped, the original page was destroyed. Her rule was that the page would first be torn into small pieces, and then the pieces mixed up and thrown down the incinerator in the hallway. She showed me how she wanted it done. She never, ever, discarded anything she had written without tearing it up completely – she didn't take whole pages, squash them up, and throw them as a ball into the wastebasket.

ARI: What about handwritten pages? Don't tell me you destroyed any of those?

MARY ANN: Oh, yes. If her changes on a handwritten page were so extensive that the page was difficult to read, she rewrote that page and gave me the original page to destroy. To tear up and incinerate.

ARI: How could you bring yourself to destroy them?

MARY ANN: Because that's what she wanted. She didn't want those pages lying around. They weren't of any use to her. She wasn't like some artists who save every scrap of paper they touch. She was concerned with the finished product, not with the process.

ARI: But this is an historic document we are talking about! Didn't you want to keep the pages as souvenirs? How many of those pages were there?

MARY ANN: I don't remember the exact number, but there were not a great many. It never occurred to me to ask for them. I think that would have been the height of presumption. And, had I asked, I think she would have been annoyed and refused. And rightly so. The one time I attempted to save a souvenir, she intervened.

ARI: What was that?

MARY ANN: Ayn paid me by check, and one day when I was depositing a few checks from her, the bank clerk recognized Ayn's name and asked me how I could bear to give them up. The clerk, I learned, was a fan. So, I decided to save a check; it was a small amount, under $10.00. A few weeks later, Ayn learned that it had not been deposited and asked me if I were saving it for a souvenir. It was clear by her manner that she did not like the idea.

ARI: What did she say?

MARY ANN: As usual, she had reasons for her reaction. One was that if I didn't cash the check, then I was not being paid for my work. And that amounted to altruism. And second, it was a nuisance to her to have checks outstanding in the account.

ARI: You said there were three house rules.

MARY ANN: The third one was never to open a window, even if Frisco was not in the room. They were concerned that he might jump out. This was a strict rule, and not just for Frisco. Later, there were other cats in the household, and the same rule applied.

ARI: Let's talk about Frisco.

MARY ANN: Frisco was a pampered, beautiful cat. Frank brushed him regularly and always spoke gently to him. Often when Ayn was reclining on the couch, Frisco would stretch out on her chest, put his paws up to her neck, and purr. She loved that.

In the morning, if Frank was still sleeping and Frisco was up and ready for breakfast, he would jump on the bed and stroke Frank's cheek to awaken him. Ayn loved to watch that, too. Frisco was allowed to use the couch to sharpen his claws; they didn't mind that the furniture had ragged ends!

ARI: You said he was involved with *Atlas Shrugged.*

MARY ANN: Frisco really demanded attention, and when he didn't get it, he would do impish things. For example, occasionally I would hear Ayn from the study saying, "Oh, no, Frisco," and then she would call for Frank or me. I'd go into the study to find Frisco on her desk, stretched out across the manuscript pages she was working on. I would pick him up and carry him out to the living room floor. Then, he would jump up to my table and stretch across the typewriter carriage! Then, I would say, "Oh, no, Frisco!" Apparently, he was known for this, because once Ayn called out, "Oh, is Frisco on your typewriter?" And when I said, "Yes," she said, "Oh, you're really being accepted now. You are one of the family." One day, I was carrying a cup of hot coffee out of the kitchen and didn't bend down to pet him when he brushed against my leg. So, he nipped my ankle and she heard me say, "Ouch, Frisco." And she said, "Oh, did Frisco bite you?" And when I answered, "Yes," she said, "That's real love. Now Frisco *really* accepts you." I should add that he never drew blood, he didn't even tear a stocking, and she knew from experience that his nips were on the gentle side.

Frisco returned their affection. Occasionally, when they were away overnight, they asked me to sleep over to keep Frisco company. The elevator door was down the hall, but you could hear it open and close. Every time that elevator door opened, Frisco would jump up and walk over to the apartment door and sit and wait. I tried to comfort him with petting and soft talk, but he wasn't interested in me. He was waiting for the sound of the key in the lock.

Once Ayn was in pain with a terrible toothache and a swollen jaw. She was standing by my typewriter, holding her cheek, and Frisco jumped up to the table, then to the top of the chair and tried to reach up to her cheek with his paw. She was very moved by that.

They were a threesome. When guests were leaving, Ayn and Frank always stood at their open door until the guests entered the elevator, and the elevator door closed. And Frisco always came and sat in front of them or beside them, to see you off.

ARI: Earlier, you mentioned having dinner with the O'Connors. Didn't they dine out?

MARY ANN: During that period, when she was completing *Atlas,* dinner was almost always at home. Sometimes she cooked it, sometimes Frank did. Being invited to dinner was the exception, not the rule. But as the work progressed, I sometimes stayed into the evening to finish up, and I was asked to stay for dinner. Especially when there was a casserole already made. Frank nick-named it the "Atlas Shrugged casserole." I don't think we ever told her about that. It was a recipe they discovered on a Mueller's macaroni box. It was delicious, quick, and easy. Frank and I prepared it a few times – macaroni, onions, hamburger, and cheese. And one casserole was dinner for three nights!

They ate simply. They did something interesting with canned peas – they were served at room temperature, mixed with mayonnaise. Once in a while, we had hamburgers from Tailor Made. She would consult Frank and me, make up the order, call it in, and then Frank and I would walk over to pick it up.

ARI: Didn't you think it a bit odd – for the author of *Atlas Shrugged* to be calling in grocery orders and hamburger orders?

MARY ANN: At first, yes, I did think so. But she never behaved as if she were the great genius who was above doing mundane things. She *was* the brilliant philosopher and writer. But if groceries and hamburgers had to be ordered, then she did that, too. She looked upon getting dinner ready as, primarily, the wife's responsibility.

ARI: Where did you eat, on the dining table that was your desk?

MARY ANN: No. Never there, because of the typewriter and supplies on it. Frank and I set up TV tables in the living room, and we ate there. If there was something interesting on TV, we watched it; otherwise, it was just friendly chat. A relaxed atmosphere.

ARI: Do you have any amusing stories centering around dining in the O'Connor household?

MARY ANN: Here's one. Early one evening, she was still working in the study. Frank and I were next door in the kitchen doing the lunch dishes and trying not to make much noise.

ARI: So as not to disturb her?

MARY ANN: That was part of it. There was something else involved. Frank explained to me that Ayn was always worried about germs. That concern started in Soviet Russia, where disease and epidemics had been constant threats. As a result, when she did the dishes, she rinsed them many times in scalding water, and insisted that Frank do the same. So, that evening, Frank said, "Let's finish these before Ayn comes in. Otherwise, we'll be here all night!" He was exaggerating, of course. But we were like two conspirators, laughing quietly about our rushing with the washing and drying. And we were discussing Leslie Howard movies we liked. Neither of us could think of "pimpernel" – as in Scarlet Pimpernel. There was a loaf of pumpernickel bread sitting on the counter, and Frank said, "I know. The Scarlet Pumpernickel." We both thought that was hilarious, and laughed out loud; and I said, "Shh, your wife is next door writing a book which is going to save the world. We had better be quiet." And Frank laughed, and said, "Well, the world will just have to wait a little while longer." And we thought that was even funnier, and broke up. And then we heard her chair scraping back on the floor. Frank said, "We're in for it now!" Followed by more muffled laughter. She walked into the kitchen, smiling, looking quizzical. "What are you two laughing at?" When we told her, she laughed, too. We apologized for disturbing her, but she said she was finished for the day. It was a cheerful moment. Then we had the casserole dinner.

ARI: What about lunch?

MARY ANN: She often took her lunch into the study and had it at her desk. It was a light lunch – sometimes just pumpernickel bread and some cheese. There's an interesting luncheon story, too.

One day, she was in the kitchen getting lunch, and I was at my typing table. She called to me, asking if I could come in and help her. I didn't know what I could do to help the author of *Atlas Shrugged*, but I was pleased by the request. I went in and saw that she was holding a hot dog, and she asked me if I thought it was edible. When I asked why, she said that it had been in the refrigerator for a while and it was shriveled. So I examined it; it was wrinkled but I pointed out that the color was good and it didn't have a bad odor. So, I told her that if it were immersed in boiling water, it would plump up. I asked her if she wanted me to do it, and she said, "Oh, no. You have work to do." That amused me, because my work consisted of typing up *her* brilliant thoughts while *she* was going to cook a hot dog!

Some minutes later, she came out of the kitchen, holding up a plump hot dog speared by a fork. "You were right," she said, and thanked me for the suggestion. I said something to the effect of "from each according to his ability." Her immediate response was, "Check your premises!"

In the discussion that followed, I learned that the premise I had to check was my assumption that because I wasn't writing the equivalent of *Atlas Shrugged*, nothing I had to say or do was of value to her. She pointed out, on that very example, that I knew something she didn't, and that I had made her lunch possible.

ARI: Did she say "check your premises" very often?

MARY ANN: Yes, and not just to me. But, I must say, whenever she did say it to me, it was music to my ears! Because I knew that I would not get out of the house without a discussion about which premises to check, or without making arrangements to discuss the issue later or the next day. That's the way she was. Always ready to analyze and explain, to help you clarify and sharpen your thoughts, your mental processes.

ARI: You once spoke of something you called "the glorious lunch break."

MARY ANN: This refers to a discussion we had that had the greatest effect on my life. One day, I was depressed because an acquaintance had criticized me for taking pleasure in cleaning a copper-bottomed frying pan. I enjoyed cleaning it and then seeing it shine on the wall, hanging on a peg board. It was the only piece of decoration in my kitchen. I was bothered by the criticism that I was finding enjoyment in something so nonintellectual. So, I told Ayn that I was troubled by something and asked her if we could have a discussion about it. She suggested that we do it during lunch.

I told her about the incident, and she nodded in understanding. When I finished, she said, "Oh, check your premises." I told her I didn't know what premises to check. So, she led me to understand the issue by questioning me about my response to the copper pot. She pointed out that it was significant that I didn't clean it and then put it away, that I hung it up so I could look at it and enjoy its beauty. That, she said, was a rational value, and I shouldn't apologize for it. In that discussion, she explored my attitude to housework in general and learned that I didn't mind doing it, and then she led me to understand that I enjoyed the result – a polished and shined appearance to a room – and why that was a value I shouldn't apologize for. She added that I didn't expect others to accomplish that for me, which was a virtue. Then she said, "Do you know what we are doing?" I didn't know what she was getting at, and I said, "We are analyzing this situation." She said, "What we are doing, Mary Ann, we are taking ideas seriously. You are applying philosophy to your life. This is what philosophy is for." She explained the necessity of identifying your values and knowing why they are values, why you shouldn't give up a value because someone questions it, even if you can't fully explain why it is important to you. She pointed out that there was much more she could say on the subject, that she had only touched on ethics and a little bit of esthetics, but that the issue for me to understand was the importance of holding on to values. To this day, I seldom mop a floor or polish a mirror without thinking of that afternoon with Ayn Rand and of how much that discussion about values has meant to me.

ARI: What did Frank O'Connor do on these days, when she was writing?

MARY ANN: He was pursuing his interest in art. He had an easel set up in the bedroom, and he worked there. Sometimes he was out doing errands or floral arrangements. They divided up the house chores. She ordered the groceries and looked after getting their dinner. He paid the bills, did banking, and took care of dry cleaning and getting the laundry done. I learned about this arrangement when there was a bit of a domestic crisis in the household one day.

ARI: What happened?

MARY ANN: One afternoon, the doorman buzzed. I answered and he told me that there was an agent from the utilities company who had come to turn off the electricity because the bill had not been paid. Frank wasn't home. I went to the study and told Ayn. She said, "What on earth?" and told me to have the man come up. She met him in the living room, and I went back to my typewriter. I couldn't hear their conversation, but it was very short, and she went to the study to write a check.

After the man left, she sat down on the couch. She was exasperated. She said things like "How can I write anything, if this is going on? Frank didn't pay the bills. This is his responsibility. What is he thinking of?" She announced, "Frank is going to turn this place into a garret of starving artists without heat or electricity!" All the while, I was trying to keep a straight face, but I smiled a bit. And she said, "You're on Frank's side!" I tried to defend him, saying that I was sure it wasn't deliberate, that he was distracted by his interest in art, that it was understandable.

ARI: What did she say to that?

MARY ANN: She told me, in firm tones, that he had ignored three delinquent notices! I couldn't think of anything to say to that. Then she went back to her desk. Later in the afternoon, Frank came home. I was ready for fireworks.

ARI: What happened?

MARY ANN: As soon as he came in, she joined him in the bedroom. I didn't hear the conversation, but when they came out I heard the tail end. She was calling him "darling" and "cubbyhole," and reminding him of the importance of paying bills on time.

ARI: What did Mr. O'Connor say?

MARY ANN: To me he said, "Well, I hear you had some excitement here this afternoon." And he added, "Glad I missed it." He was amused by the incident. We all went back to work, and that was that.

FINISHING *ATLAS SHRUGGED*

ARI: Were you there when Miss Rand finished writing *Atlas Shrugged?*

MARY ANN: Yes, that is one of my most vivid memories.

ARI: What happened?

MARY ANN: *Atlas Shrugged* was finished on the afternoon of Wednesday, March 20, 1957. That, incidentally, is the date she wrote on the last page of the manuscript. The only people there, besides Ayn, were Frank, Joan, Leonard, and me.

At the time, Ayn was working against a deadline, a date when she was scheduled to turn in the final typed manuscript of the novel to Random House. My job was to get the typing and proof-reading finished by that deadline. I had agreed with Ayn not to let the work pile up; I was to keep up with her. On March 20, there were typewritten pages to be proofread. I had typed them earlier in the week, and I asked Joan to proofread with me. Ayn knew we were coming over.

We arrived at the apartment after lunch, about 1:00 p.m. We knew Ayn was writing the last chapter but we didn't know how close to the end she was. Frank answered the door, and said something like "I think this is going to be it, kids." Then, he went back to his easel in the bedroom.

As I said earlier, whenever I went over to do some work and she was writing, I would tap on the study door, enter, take my work, and leave. But, after hearing Frank, I decided that we should not disturb her. We sat in the living room, whispering. More than an hour passed. Finally, I thought that one of us should quietly enter the study and quickly take the manuscript pages we needed – I knew exactly where they were on the bottom shelf of the bookcase. But, which one of us?

ARI: Which one was it?

MARY ANN: Joan. How we decided that Joan should be the one is amusing. We concluded that since she was petite, she would be less noticeable! I told her to tap lightly and enter. She walked back to the study, and here is what I heard: a few taps on the study door, followed by Ayn's voice speaking in a stern manner: "If you come in here, I'll kill you." That's an exact quote.

Joan returned, and we retreated to the farthest corner of the living room and sat whispering and wondering. I decided to call Leonard and tell him what was happening. I had to go down to the lobby to use the pay phone, because the only telephone in the apartment was in Ayn's study. Leonard lived a few blocks away, and he came right over. He joined us in the corner of the living room, and we three whispered and waited. I'm not sure how much time passed; it seemed like hours, but it wasn't. And then we heard the loveliest sound in the world – Ayn's chair scraping against the wooden floor. We heard her footsteps walking out of the study, we heard Frank say, "Congratulations, darling." Then we heard her walking into the living room. She entered, dressed in a skirt and short-sleeved blouse, her hair was somewhat disheveled, her face was a little shiny. She was walking toward us, holding up a manuscript page with her thumb and index finger. We approached her and read the words "The End" at the bottom of the page. She looked young, she was smiling broadly, her eyes were bright. Frank followed her in, and he was beaming.

ARI: Was she angry about the interruption?

MARY ANN: She didn't even mention it. After hugs and congratulations, we apologized for disturbing her. She dismissed it with a wave of her hand. She said it was all right, that we had no way of knowing what page she was on. She was so happy in those moments, I don't think anything could have undercut her joy at having finished *Atlas*. She wanted to have the Collective[1] over that night to celebrate. Then we left. It was still daylight.

ARI: How did you celebrate?

MARY ANN: We had champagne. The "If you come in here, I'll kill you" story was told, to everyone's amusement. Ayn said that she didn't know who was tapping on the study door. We had coffee and pastries. I remember picking up some at the bakery on Third Avenue that the O'Connors used, Versailles Patisserie.

ARI: Were there any pictures taken, just after she finished writing the last page?

MARY ANN: Right after she finished? No. No one had a camera. If we'd had a camera, we would have snapped her as she walked into the living room holding up the last page!

ARI: Do you remember typing the last page?

MARY ANN: I typed only part of it. As I was typing the last chapter, Ayn said I could type everything but the last lines. She wanted to type those herself. When that time came, she sat down at the typewriter and said that even though she was a fast typist, she made a lot of mistakes. She added that she better not make any this time. So she typed, very slowly, from "He raised his hand…." to "The End." After she finished, she said, "Now it *really* does say 'The End.'"

---

[1] "The Collective" was Ayn Rand's tongue-in-cheek name for a small group that met on Saturday nights to discuss her works and philosophy.

Chapter II

Ayn Rand and Charles Sures

MEETING AYN RAND

ARI: Charles, when did you meet Ayn Rand?

CHARLES: February 1960, in New York City. Branden was giving lectures on Objectivism, and I knew that she came for the question period to answer questions. At the end of the evening, I went up to the podium, and I introduced myself. But we didn't have a conversation. Some of her friends were there. They were going out for coffee, and I was invited along. The next thing I knew, I was walking down the street and talking with Ayn Rand.

ARI: How did it happen that you were walking with her?

CHARLES: As we were leaving, people broke up into couples, and I saw that she was walking with Frank. There was this whole side of Ayn Rand unoccupied, and so I hurried over to fill the gap.

ARI: What do you remember of that meeting?

CHARLES: I remember that what happened surprised me. I was glowing inwardly at my good fortune. At most, I had expected to introduce myself that evening, maybe have a brief conversation, and then leave. But, there I was, walking with her! I was thinking of what to say. But *she* took over, and began the conversation. I thought she would want to talk about the lecture or some aspect of the philosophy. But no, she was interested in *me* – who I was, what I did for a living. When I told her that I was an attorney and had come from Washington, D.C., to hear her, she smiled and said it was a compliment to her that I had come "so far," and it indicated a serious interest in ideas. She wanted to know what aspect of the law I specialized in and what I enjoyed about my work. It was the focus on me that I hadn't expected. You would have thought that *I* was the celebrity.

ARI: What were your impressions of her?

CHARLES: In manner, she was a very gracious lady. I would say she was friendly, but not familiar.

ARI: Would you say she was formal?

CHARLES: No, formal is too strong a word. I'd characterize it as more of a cordial reserve. There was a respectful distance, but there was also civility and an attitude of good will. I believed that she was genuinely interested in me. Frank was that way, too.

I don't remember what else we talked about. At one point, she was speaking and we were about to cross a street. She started to step off the curb – without looking. I took her arm to stop her and she looked up at me; she seemed a little surprised. But I had the impression she approved of the protective gesture. I also remember that she went right on speaking to make her point, as if there hadn't been an interruption. That, I learned, was typical of her: nothing distracted her; she never lost her train of thought. She never paused to say things like "What were we talking about?" or "Where was I?" She always knew.

ARI: Did you see her after that?

CHARLES: I saw her whenever I could. I traveled to where she was speaking – Philadelphia, Boston, New York. In fact, she was there when I met Mary Ann. In 1962 Ayn gave a lecture at Hunter College where Mary Ann was teaching. I knew who Mary Ann was, but she didn't know me. After the lecture, I followed Ayn and her friends into an elevator, and Mary Ann and I were introduced. But I didn't get to know Ayn on a personal basis until I started to date Mary Ann the following year and went to social gatherings attended by Ayn and Frank. That was really the beginning of my relationship with Ayn.

STAMP COLLECTING

ARI: Charles, at the U.S. Post Office ceremony introducing the Ayn Rand stamp, you gave a short speech about stamp collecting with Miss Rand. Did she get you interested in stamps and collecting?

CHARLES: Actually, she revived my interest in stamps with the article she wrote for the *Minkus Stamp Journal* in 1971 – "Why I Like Stamp Collecting."[1] It got me into *collecting* stamps again, instead of just accumulating them.

ARI: How do you mean?

CHARLES: Until I read that article, I had the mistaken notion that stamp collecting was a nonintellectual endeavor for children. I had a stamp collection when I was a child, but over the years I drifted away from organized collecting habits. I stopped putting stamps into albums. I had a box in which I put the stamps I liked personally, that's all. Then I read the article and my return to collecting began. She explained the many ways in which that hobby was a legitimate intellectual and enjoyable pursuit for an adult. It liberated me, and opened up a world of pleasure.

ARI: How did you get involved with stamp collecting with Miss Rand?

CHARLES: It was gradual. My intent was to collect the dozen or so of her favorite stamps that were illustrated in the article, and

---

[1] Reprinted in Peter Schwartz (ed.), *The Ayn Rand Column*, Second Renaissance Books, 1998

LAW OFFICES
CHARLES SURES
SUITE 607 METROPOLITAN BUILDING
8720 GEORGIA AVENUE
SILVER SPRING, MARYLAND 20910

ELIZABETH H. FARQUHAR

WHITFORD W. CHESTON
VIRGINIA ASSOCIATE

TELEPHONE 587-3434

January 29, 1973

Dear Ayn,

Enclosed are:

I have it — 507	$ 2.50	
499	.30 *yes*	
I have it — 26	5.00	
I have it — 503	1.75	
no — 484	2.50	
I have it — 319	3.50	
550	2.25 — *yes*	
299	7.00 — *yes*	
296	10.00 — *yes*	
294	2.10 — *yes*	
TOTAL	$27.00	
	36.90	

Keep any, all or none. I inadvertently bought many of these
as duplicates. No. 26, while only "fine", is a beautiful
color.

All are <u>good</u> prices - exactly what I paid for them. Some at
wholesale, some at low retail.

And: cheers for your compliments to the Apollo Program in
your latest Letter and, also, cheers for you. After all,
you were first to the moon in philosophy; so the greatest
compliment to the Apollo men is praise from you.

March 9-11 is Interpex. I'll call you when the time draws
close.

A hug for you both from us both.

carried forward $27.00
"*Love*" P.B. + Sgl. .56
O'Neil L.P. + Sgl 3.—
$30.56

Charles

Paid 2/23/73

to do no more than that. But once I had collected her page of stamps, I was completely in thrall. When I told her what I had done, she was delighted and encouraged me to continue. Soon after that, we became fellow collectors, in earnest.

ARI: What did this involve?

CHARLES: One project involved a collection I had purchased at an estate sale – twenty stamp albums, each album of a different country, about 20,000 stamps in all. I got it at a very good price. Actually, I didn't get it for myself. I bought it so she and I could have some fun with it. She collected worldwide, I only collected American, so it suited her interests.

ARI: Did she buy them from you?

CHARLES: Individual stamps, yes, but not whole albums. Our agreement was that I would deliver a few albums to her, she would select the stamps she needed, and I would then take back these albums and replace them with a few more. This went on for about a year and a half. She was scrupulous about keeping records and paying me for the stamps she bought. She carefully marked which stamps she had taken, or made a list. I kept a running account of what she owed me and would bill her from time to time.

ARI: How did you arrive at the price?

CHARLES: We agreed on two cents a stamp, as a general rule, based on what I had paid for the collection. But if we thought that the value of a particular stamp was significantly higher, she used the catalog value as a guide to decide upon a price higher than two cents.

It was a real bargain, the way I figured it. I broke even on the investment except for the million bucks worth of pleasure I got from our discussions and negotiations, and from knowing that I helped her acquire about fifteen hundred stamps for her collection.

ARI: How large was her collection?

CHARLES: By 1974 she had about 45,000 stamps, all of which she knew from memory. She was phenomenal in that regard.

She knew exactly what she owned, and she never mistakenly bought a duplicate. She kept an exact count of her collection, and whenever I asked she had a figure at hand. The last count was something more than 52,000 stamps. It was a worldwide collection, but she would not, and did not, collect stamps from communist countries.

ARI: Was her collection distinguished in any particular way?

CHARLES: Yes and no. It was not unique, but it was vast. In terms of size, it was out of the ordinary. And it was so well kept it was a pleasure to casually leaf through it. But it was not particularly valuable, which resulted from her approach to stamp collecting.

ARI: What was that?

CHARLES: She did not collect for investment, as some philatelists do. They insist on the best quality and they search for rare stamps, all with the expectation that the value of the collection will increase. Ayn collected for keeps and never intended to sell. She was not a stickler for perfect quality in stamps, but they had to be more than merely presentable. They had to be good-looking and above-average quality – not faded or torn. She acquired both unused and used stamps, but she preferred the unused ones.

When she first started filling up albums, she attached the stamps to an album page with special hinges that required physically gluing the stamps to the page. Later, she used mounts which held the stamps securely in place without gluing. This practice preserved the mint condition of unused stamps. Like all dedicated stamp collectors, she was concerned with preserving and presenting her collection in the best, most attractive way possible. She was very proud of it. If she had added many new stamps to an album, or if she had completed a page, she brought it out to show me. She never tired of going through an album and commenting on particular stamps. Her enthusiasm never waned.

ARI: Besides the twenty albums, did you help her acquire other stamps?

CHARLES: Sure. I attended more stamp shows than she did, and before I went to one, I would check in with her to see if there was anything she wanted. She would give me a list of stamps she needed and the price range for each one. I made a number of purchases for her over the years and kept up the accounting. There were times when I purchased a stamp she didn't have and which a good collection should have, but which was expensive. I would tell her that if she didn't want it, I would keep it in my collection. I meant it, even though the stamp was a duplicate of one I owned. But she always bought it.

ARI: Did you give her any stamps as gifts?

CHARLES: Yes, but at her insistence we agreed that I could not spend more than two dollars on a stamp gift for her. As a general rule, Ayn did not like to receive gifts from admirers, and it was her policy to return a gift if she had not met the person or knew that person only casually. She said that accepting a gift created an implied obligation upon her to reciprocate, and she thought it an "enormous" — one of her favorite adjectives – presumption, especially if she had not met the person sending the gift.

ARI: So accepting two-dollar stamp gifts from you was an exception?

CHARLES: A very happy exception. And it was one way of reciprocating for the times I stayed overnight at the O'Connors' when in town for a stamp show or other business.

ARI: We'll have to talk about those overnighters. But, first, tell me about Miss Rand and the stamp shows.

CHARLES: There were two large shows in New York City, one in the spring and one in the fall, and we tried to make it to at least one of them, and some years we went to both. Over the years, Ayn and Frank did not initiate many phone calls. Mary Ann and I did most of the calling. But she never failed to call about the date of a stamp show and make arrangements to go if she could.

They were all-day affairs and could be tiring. There were hundreds of booths and tables for the dealers, and thousands of people attended. But she was a trooper; she had the stamina. She said she found that just being there was energizing.

She approached a stamp show in a very business-like way.

She always came prepared with a list of what she needed. Also, she had a stamp budget. On the way to a show, she would declare a budget limit – usually around three hundred dollars. But if she found a stamp that exceeded her budget, she would pause, look at me, and ask, "Should I?" I always said, "Yes," whereupon she treated herself to it with a kind of resigned sigh of pleasure – as if she were succumbing to the irresistible. Like all collectors, she went over budget. But I can't recall any stamp purchase over four hundred dollars.

When we entered a show, we were given name tags to wear, and she always wrote "Ayn Rand" on hers, not "Ayn O'Connor." She was proud of being a stamp collector and wanted to go as the author of her article on stamp collecting.

ARI: Was her name recognized?

CHARLES: In all the stamp shows we went to, it was recognized only once. But she didn't mind. She said that it meant that people there were concerned with stamps, not with celebrities, and that's the way it should be. She liked the atmosphere of camaraderie and good will at these shows.

ARI: How do you mean?

CHARLES: People there were motivated by a value they held in common – the love of stamps. She said you could see it in so many forms: dealers had their wares neatly arranged, a few dealers remembered her from previous years and were happy to see her again. She saw people studying stamps intently. They were people with a purpose, she said. There was only one occasion when the good will was lacking.

ARI: What was that?

CHARLES: At one show, she was examining an attractive stamp at a dealer's booth. When he saw that she was interested in it, he brought out several examples to show her. When she indicated that she was not in the market for the stamp at that time, he got impatient and brusque in manner. Ayn was silent for a few seconds and then she looked up and quietly asked, "Have I offended you?" The dealer was embarrassed and apologized and became a gentleman again. His behavior was an exception to the pleasant atmosphere, but it was jarring. This incident led to a discussion with Ayn that I found touching.

ARI: Tell me about it.

CHARLES: A few hours later, Ayn and I were having hamburgers and coffee. I noticed a slight frown in her expression, and I asked if anything was troubling her. She acknowledged that she felt a little depressed, and I asked why. She said she was not sure at the moment. I asked if it was caused by the rudeness of the dealer, and she said she didn't think so. Then she expressed appreciation for my trying to help. She said she appreciated it because I wasn't treating her as if she were from the stratosphere, that I didn't back away from the situation on account of her being who she was. Then she asked me if it troubled me to see her get down over something. I assured her that it didn't. And she added that it was a change from her usual role, where she was the one bolstering someone else's spirits.

ARI: Did she ever say what was troubling her?

CHARLES: No, and I never inquired. She never raised the subject again, and that meant that she didn't want to talk about it. I felt free to discuss anything with her except matters which I considered were entirely private to her or were entirely private to me. Ayn respected privacy. She didn't probe into areas of your private life, and she expected you to keep out of hers.

ARI: Did that incident undercut her pleasure in stamps that day?

CHARLES: No. At every stamp show, we both made purchases – of stamps, or souvenir sheets, or supplies. And the first thing she wanted to do when we got home that day was to unpack her purchases and show them to Frank. She was happy.

ARI: Did Mr. O'Connor ever go to the stamp shows? Or Mary Ann?

CHARLES: No. They weren't interested the way Ayn and I were. I shared Ayn's attitude, that stamp shows were for dedicated enthusiasts, not onlookers. So Frank and Mary Ann weren't invited.

ARI: What did they do while you were gone?

CHARLES: If Mary Ann was in town with me, she and Frank would spend the day doing what they enjoyed. They liked to stroll around New York and window shop, or go to a department store and browse through the home decorating department. But after a show, the four of us would have dinner together. Ayn always wanted a report from Frank about what *he* did that day.

On many occasions, when Ayn and I were leaving for the day, Frank would say, "They're off stampeding again!"

ARI: You once wrote to Miss Rand in response to her inquiry about the possibility that some stamps she bought might be counterfeit. What was the outcome of this?

CHARLES: Ayn had a set of U.S. stamps known as the Kansas-Nebraska overprints. Counterfeiters found it easy to print the name of the state on the plain original issues to make them appear as the specially authorized over-print stamps. Experts can tell the genuine from the false, and Ayn wanted this assurance; they ruled her stamps genuine.

ARI: Did Miss Rand ever give you a gift of stamps?

CHARLES: We didn't exchange gifts, except for small hostess gifts that Mary Ann and I would take over. But she did select two stamps that our friends, including Ayn and Frank, gave me for my fiftieth birthday. Mary Ann gave me a party in New York at Joan and Allan's apartment. All our friends chipped in, and Mary Ann asked Ayn to select the stamps. Ayn knew what my collection lacked, and purchased two rare stamps in perfect condition from Jacques Minkus, the famous stamp dealer.

She was delightful that evening. During the party, she asked me to sit on the couch near her. She then announced to all present that she had gone over my latest accounting for stamps and found that I had made a ten-dollar error in her favor. She produced a ten dollar bill and, waving it with a flourish, made this light-hearted comment, "It's a good thing I'm honest." And I love the greeting she wrote on the group birthday card.

ARI: Which is?

CHARLES: "Happy Stampeding!"

AYN RAND AS HOSTESS

ARI: Let's talk about those overnight stays. What was a visit to Miss Rand like?

CHARLES: She jokingly called me her "corner tenant." She explained that in communist Russia, living quarters were at a premium, so much so that a person who had an apartment could rent the four corners of a room to tenants. So I became her "corner tenant" – without paying rent, of course.

Ayn took seriously being a hostess. She made sure her housekeeper had everything ready for my stay. She pointed out the fresh towels in the guest bathroom; there was always a fresh bar of soap; she reminded me of the juice and sandwiches in the refrigerator.

There was an amusing ritual. She explained that the cats, being mischievous, were not permitted in the living room overnight. Their seclusion was guaranteed by implementing what she jokingly designated "the decompression chamber."

ARI: What was that?

CHARLES: A long hallway connecting the living room with the master bedroom. There were doors at each end. The cats stayed in the bedroom and were prevented from escaping into the living room by the policy of never having both doors to the "decompression chamber" open at the same time. This saved her and Frank from chasing cats. The guest bathroom and her study were off this chamber, and if I entered it I had to make sure there weren't any cats in it waiting to escape. "All clear," Ayn, Frank, and I would call out from time to time.

ARI: When you were there, did she cook?

CHARLES: She might make coffee or tea, but not meals. Either we ate out or dinner was prepared and served by Eloise.[1] I know that Ayn supplied many of the recipes.

ARI: What was a typical dinner like?

CHARLES: In service, it was formal in the sense that the table was completely set and Ayn had a crystal bell at her place to summon Eloise, which she did between courses. Ayn sat at the head of the table, with Frank opposite her. Even though we might all be in casual clothes, dinner was genteel. There was an elegance to the occasion.

ARI: What was served?

CHARLES: Complete dinners, usually with salad as an appetizer and a main course, with vegetables. One of their favorite dishes was beef Stroganoff, made from a recipe Ayn had brought from Russia, and that was served a few times. One year, Mary Ann and I were there a week before Thanksgiving. Ayn had Eloise prepare a complete Thanksgiving dinner with turkey and all the trimmings, and we all celebrated in advance of the holiday. There was always coffee or tea and dessert, which was usually several flavors of ice cream and often a Russian nut cake made by Eloise. Ayn always made sure that Frank, who was on the thin side, had balanced, nutritious meals.

During the evening, Frank or Ayn made coffee and served it with miniature Danish pastries or cookies. And there were always soft drinks available, your choice of Coca-Cola or Pepsi. Their guests were well taken care of.

There were times when Mary Ann and I spent the afternoon with Ayn and Frank on an outing but were not going to stay for dinner. On the way back to their apartment, Ayn and Frank always stopped at the delicatessen in the building and purchased some cold cuts for a snack for us before we left.

---

[1] Eloise Huggins was the O'Connors' longtime cook and housekeeper.

ARI: What were evenings like after dinner?

CHARLES: I enjoyed talks that lasted into the early morning hours. Ayn was not indefatigable, but I never met anyone who outlasted her. She might get tired, and she might unabashedly yawn, but she was never the first to call an end to the evening. Frank usually turned in before we did. If I yawned, she would say, "OK, that's it," and we would call it a night. She would tell me to help myself to anything I wanted in the refrigerator. And she would then proceed to make up the couch with sheets, pillow, and blanket. I told her that *I* would make up the couch, but she always insisted on doing it as a service, she said, for her "corner tenant." I never got used to her doing chores like that. I never forgot who she was and what she had accomplished.

As a guest, I have a special recollection of a January 1. We had been to a New Year's Eve party, and Mary Ann and I drove them home. We had planned to drop them off and go directly home to Maryland, where I had to prepare for a trial. They expressed concern about the five-hour drive, and they urged us to come up with them for a rest and a bite to eat before our journey, which we did. Now, the living room windows of their apartment looked down on 34th Street, where I had parked the car across from their building. We said our goodbyes, which included their admonitions to drive carefully, to stop and rest at diners, and so on. We walked to our car and looked up and there they were, Ayn and Frank, standing at the window, making sure we got into our car safely, and waving to us. It was an endearing sight.

AYN RAND AS CLIENT

ARI: Charles, you were one of Miss Rand's attorneys. What was she like as a client?

CHARLES: Her main attorneys were in New York City, but in the early sixties, I handled a few matters for her. When it came to discussing legal matters, her manner was completely professional. Her tone was impersonal, almost as if she were not acquainted with you. Her focus was on the issue at hand and how it affected her.

ARI: We've seen in the archives some of your legal correspondence which Miss Rand had reviewed. Was this customary?

CHARLES: When I represented her, she went over letters I wrote. She was a hands-on client. She didn't sit back and let her lawyers take over. She wanted to know what legal issues were involved and what were her rights. She wanted to be consulted before action was taken. Not that she wanted to direct every aspect of a case. She knew that her attorneys had legal expertise she didn't have, and she respected that. But she thought it was her responsibility to know what action was being taken and why.

ARI: Let's talk about the letters.

CHARLES: The very first letter I wrote for her was to an adversary, and it concerned the misappropriation of the names of characters in her novels. It was a good letter from a legal standpoint; it made all the right points. When I reviewed it with Ayn, she complimented me on the opening sentence, but asked if the next sentence could be changed as to a word or two and the juxtaposition of a clause. It sounded good to me so, of course, I agreed. We made other changes. When I got back to my office in Maryland and dictated the revised letter, I found that the only part of it that remained word for word from the original was the first sentence! Her editorial changes gave the letter a greater clarity and brought the issues into sharper focus.

ARI: What was her manner during the editing process?

CHARLES: Whenever she suggested a revision, she gave reasons for it, no matter how small the change. She was open to discussion; if I disagreed, she listened and we talked it out. She took her time and gave you time to think. I never felt pressured.

Shortly after that, I wrote a couple of lengthy letters on a libel matter. She approved the letters, which resulted in an effective conclusion to the case.

ARI: What case was that?

CHARLES: It was the debacle of the showing of *The Fountainhead* film in Portland, Oregon. In October 1963, Ayn received an honorary degree of Doctor of Humane Letters from Lewis and Clark College in Portland. I was not with her, but I was doing some legal work for her at that time.

ARI: What happened?

CHARLES: During the two days of special presentations of her works, in tribute to her as philosopher and writer, *The Fountainhead* was shown as part of the honors and ceremonies. The rented film had been cut and distorted, contrary to the assurance that the film shown would be the uncut original. Ayn stopped the film when it became apparent that Roark's speech to the jury had been omitted. She gave an extemporaneous condemnation of the wrong that had been perpetrated.

ARI: What was your involvement?

CHARLES: I did some research on Oregon libel law. Then I wrote to the film company demanding, among other relief, that the uncut version be provided for showing at the college. Lewis and

Clark College was innocent of any fault in the matter. The film company advised that although the cuts were made without their knowledge, they would make amends immediately, and they did so. As a result, Ayn wrote to the president of Lewis and Clark College regarding a date for the showing, saying, "I am anxious to have the full film shown at Lewis and Clark College in order to correct the disgraceful impression made by the censored version."

ARI: You've said she was a "hands-on" client. Did that make it harder or easier to deal with her?

CHARLES: Easier, without a doubt. It was clear she had done considerable thinking before we discussed legal matters – so she saved us time, which was important to both of us.

When Mary Ann had the art reproduction company, I prepared the contracts by which Ayn and Frank gave the company the exclusive rights to reproduce both Ilona's[1] portrait of Ayn and Frank's painting, *Diminishing Returns.* Ayn was very experienced with contracts. She was an old pro, you could say. This was apparent in the one modification she requested in her contract – the right to have the portrait reproduced on book jackets and/or in periodicals. Otherwise the contracts were signed as written.

ARI: Did being friends make the process easier?

CHARLES: Being friends never entered into it. She was focused on whether the contracts protected her and Frank's interests. It was strictly business. That's what made it a pleasure.

---

[1] Artist Ilona Royce Smithkin

Chapter III

Ayn Rand as Mentor

CONVERSATIONS WITH MARY ANN

ARI: Mary Ann, you must have had many conversations with Miss Rand.

MARY ANN: Many. Some long, some short, on a wide range of topics – from current events to psycho-epistemology to women's clothing. These conversations came about in different ways. Something I said would lead her to inquire further. Very often, something she had written or lectured about prompted questions from me. Over the years, the same subject was discussed in different contexts – if she had made a new identification or defined a new principle, for example. And there were group discussions, too. So, now – years later – it's not possible for me to separate the content of most individual conversations from her writings and speeches and other discussions – the knowledge is all integrated. But I do remember highlights of conversations that had special, personal meaning for me, that were focused on my questions and concerns.

ARI: Let's talk about those. Did you take notes? Is that one of the reasons you remember them?

MARY ANN: No. The first time we had an appointment to discuss an issue, I came with a notebook, prepared to take notes. But she asked me not to.

ARI: What were her reasons?

MARY ANN: That it was not possible for me to follow her train of thought, ask questions, and take notes – at the same time. At first, I was surprised and disappointed, but as the evening progressed I could see that she was right. It took all of my mental energy to focus on her explanations and follow her reasoning. Everything she said was relevant and to the point. Note taking would have been a hindrance to understanding.

ARI: Was that always her policy?

MARY ANN: In my experience, yes. Except if she were giving a course, such as the lectures on fiction writing. Then note taking was permitted because it was a classroom setup and she was teaching. But, in our private conversations, she wanted my full attention. At the end of a discussion, she would always invite further discussion at a later time if, after reviewing the issues, I had more questions. And during the discussion, she invited questions, too.

In those early days, as soon as I got home after an evening with her, I made notes of everything I could remember. So that I could think about it, make sure I understood it, and jot down questions if I didn't.

Our very first conversation after the oral exam had to do with teaching. It was the winter of 1955. At the time, I was giving a medieval art course at NYU, and I personally did not like most of the art – the flatness, the distortions in anatomy, the vacant, staring faces. I asked if it is proper to express my personal likes or dislikes when teaching.

ARI: What did she have to say to that?

MARY ANN: She said she was going to begin by asking me a question. Then she did something that was characteristic of her in any discussion: she got right to the heart of the issue. This is almost verbatim: "Tell me," she asked, "What were you hired to teach?" She stressed the word "hired." And I answered that the course was supposed to cover the history and development of subject and style in medieval art. Then she asked me two questions: was there anything about the subject that required me to express my personal opinions; and did such opinions clarify or add to the understanding of the history of medieval art? Well, of course, the answer was "no" to both. And she said, well, if that's the case, why do you want to include them?

I didn't know why and couldn't say. But I could see that she was right. I wondered out loud why I was ever confused about the issue in the first place. Now, I didn't expect an answer; to me, that was a rhetorical question. But not to Ayn Rand! She picked up on it immediately, and said that that was a separate question, an issue we could pursue if there was time. But, first, she said, she wanted to state a principle.

ARI: What was that?

MARY ANN: In any endeavor, in order to determine whether an action is appropriate, you have to define your purpose, you have to know what goal you want to achieve. And she gave a few simple examples to make her point. I remember only one – that if your goal is to lose weight, then you should stay away from fattening foods like cake and ice cream. And then she applied the principle to my case. If my goal was to present the history and development of medieval art, my personal reactions were not necessary. But, she said, suppose that part of the teaching assignment was to cover changing estimates of medieval art over time; then it would be appropriate to include mine as an illustration of a certain viewpoint.

ARI: But suppose a student asks for your opinion; can't you give it?

MARY ANN: She was way ahead of us! She raised and answered that question, too. If a student asks for your estimate and response to medieval art, then it is appropriate for you to give it, *if you want to.* But only if you want to. It is optional. Here she made another important point.

ARI: Which was?

MARY ANN: That if I did give my personal views on medieval art, then I should indicate the reasons why I held those views. That way, she said, you are communicating the idea that there are reasons for esthetic responses, that they are not causeless emotions. However, she cautioned me to keep those comments to a minimum, and to answer those inquiries after the day's lesson was finished. To keep my personal views out of the course material.

She frowned on professors who mix their personal views with their presentation of the subject, so that the students have a difficult, if not impossible, time separating the two. She said it put an unnecessary mental burden on the students.

ARI: What was her manner throughout all this?

MARY ANN: Just like she was during the oral exam. Completely focused on the issue and on my understanding of it – stopping to make sure I understood a point before going on to the next one. And something else, too. She was aware not only of what I was thinking, but of what I was feeling. She commented on the change she noticed in my facial expression and posture as the evening progressed. I was tense when we began; I looked troubled; I was sitting up straight. But, as I began to understand the issue, the worried look left my face, and I sat back in a much more relaxed manner. She was aware of all this. Whenever I was with her, I always knew I was being seen and heard.

In fact, some years later, one of our conversations resulted from her noticing my emotional state one evening.

ARI: Talk about that.

MARY ANN: She observed that I looked troubled, and asked me what was wrong. At the time, I was unhappy about a career problem, and I told her what it was. And I added that I was down on myself for feeling as I did. That last comment was what generated the discussion. But first we discussed the career problem, what caused it, and the possible solutions. We concluded that I didn't have any choice in the matter. She pointed out that I was about to lose a value, and that that was reason enough to be unhappy. So, she asked, why do you hold that against yourself, why are you critical of yourself for feeling as you do? That was what had to be identified. And here she made an eye-opening point.

ARI: Which was?

MARY ANN: She said that the fact that happiness is the moral purpose of your life doesn't mean that you must never be unhappy. Or, put another way, unhappiness isn't necessarily caused by immorality, and one shouldn't equate the two. Then she elaborated.

ARI: What points did she make?

MARY ANN: Well, first she reviewed the relationship between happiness and values – that the former results from the achievement of the latter. Then she said it was important to realize and accept that we cannot always control the events and circumstances that affect our values. As an example, she gave what she considered the worst possible case – the death of a spouse. Another example she gave was losing a job because of a recession in the economy. Or having a friend go back on his word. We can't prevent these things, she said, yet they affect us. She gave herself as an example – when *The Fountainhead* was being rejected by publishers, she was not happy.

She went on. If a person is chronically unhappy and depressed, regardless of the circumstances in his life, then there is something wrong psychologically, and the person should seek professional help. But if the unhappiness results from the loss of a value and the person is not responsible, then there should be no self-recrimination. Here she made another distinction.

ARI: What was that?

MARY ANN: When things go wrong in your life, you will be unhappy. But the important question at those times is: are you at peace with yourself? That, she said, is something that *is* within your control. And when people don't make this distinction, they suffer unnecessarily.

ARI: Can you elaborate? What does being at peace with yourself come from?

MARY ANN: From the knowledge that you did not betray your values, that you lived up to your standards to the best of your ability. From knowing that whatever mistakes you might have made, they were *honest* mistakes, they did not come from the refusal to think. That you are free from the nagging thought: if only I had done thus and so, things might be different. That you know you did not let yourself down, that your self-esteem is intact. That you lived up to the best within you. Then you are at peace with yourself.

ARI: How did this conversation affect you?

MARY ANN: It made all the difference in the world to me. I still had the career problem, but I could localize it, confine it, see it in perspective. I went there feeling burdened by some kind of great weight. At the end of the evening, I felt free of the un-named burden. She had named it.

ARI: Was there a time when Miss Rand didn't welcome questions?

MARY ANN: No, never. If she couldn't discuss something because of her work and deadlines, she would ask you to be sure and raise the subject again, or call and make an appointment. Whenever I did call and say I had a question or an issue to discuss, she would always ask me to indicate the issue. Then we would make an appointment. Then she would always say, "Take it as far as you can by yourself, before we get together." She wanted it to be a joint effort.

When we did get together, the sessions could last for hours. If we began at 8:00 p.m., I might not leave until 2:00 in the morning, or even later. And sometimes the discussion would be continued the next day by phone, if she had the time. What I just related were *highlights* of discussions. In answering any question, she pursued *every* aspect – every implication, every relevant connection to related issues, every necessary qualification. She questioned you, she gave examples; she posed clarifying alternatives. It was an exhaustive treatment of the issue. But it was not exhausting! Just the opposite. It was invigorating.

ARI: Would you clarify that last statement?

MARY ANN: In order to follow her progression of thought, you had to stay in full focus all the time. She didn't wander mentally, so you didn't either. She was like a ray of light moving ahead at a steady pace, and you tried to keep up with that light and see everything it illuminated. You stretched your brain. You tried to rise to her level of mental functioning. As a result, you were a better person for having been with her, for having made that effort.

I lived a few blocks away, but if I were leaving after midnight she always cautioned me not to walk home, but to have the doorman get me a cab. I did, but I really didn't want to. I loved the times when it was early enough to walk home. I left her feeling exhilarated. It was like being on a mental high. And I didn't want to come down. My mind had been in motion and I didn't want to stop the movement. Exploring an issue with Ayn Rand was like climbing a moving escalator, two steps at a time. You reached your goal faster. I wanted to prolong that sensation of moving forward and up – to swing my arms, take longer steps and deeper breaths. That's what she made possible.

DISCUSSING ART

ARI: Miss Rand had very definite preferences in art. Reading *The Romantic Manifesto*, I see that she admired Vermeer and disliked Rembrandt. Did she ever discuss your art preferences with you, Mary Ann?

MARY ANN: She had very definite preferences in everything. As far as my own preferences, we did discuss them on a number of occasions. And I always found those discussions valuable. I always learned something – not only about the subject, but about myself, about what I liked and why I liked it. I can give you an example. But first I want to clear up something about Miss Rand and Rembrandt, since you mentioned him.

ARI: What's that?

MARY ANN: She didn't admire some of his subjects or his painterly style. She made that clear in her writing and in lectures, and she gave her reasons. But she did acknowledge, to me personally and during question periods publicly, that he was masterful in his use of light and dark, in his way of composing with those elements to achieve arresting and dramatic effects. In her appraisal of him, she made this distinction.

Some people who admired Rembrandt were offended by her remarks. But, I often wonder if they ever discussed with her what they liked about him and why, and explored their responses. The times I discussed art preferences with her, I learned how to approach something critically in a way I hadn't been able to do before the discussion.

ARI: Give me an example.

MARY ANN: It was a discussion about the movie *The African Queen*, starring Katherine Hepburn and Humphrey Bogart. At the time, it was one of my favorite movies. More than once, I praised it and recommended it to Ayn and Frank, who hadn't seen it. I knew they liked Hepburn.

ARI: Why did you like it?

MARY ANN: I thought it was a great adventure story about ordinary people who undertake to do something extraordinary. I liked the effect that Hepburn and Bogart had on one another. He was a drunk and a coward, and she encouraged him to be brave and sober. She was a repressed, compliant, and very proper spinster; and with him she became assertive, feminine, and a woman in love. They brought out the best in each other. They were in a terrible situation, had to fight for survival, and they didn't give up. And, most important, they succeeded.

ARI: So what happened?

MARY ANN: One day – this was after the publication of *Atlas* – Ayn called me to say that *The African Queen* was playing on television that evening, and invited me over to watch it with them. I thought they would see the same things in it that I did and would like it, too. Well, very early in the movie, she began to indicate her disapproval, and so did Frank, but not as much as she did. And my heart sank.

ARI: What didn't she approve of? How did she indicate it?

MARY ANN: The pronounced naturalistic touches in the movie. For example, in the scene where they are having tea, Bogart's stomach is making growling and gurgling noises. And she thought Hepburn was made to look unnecessarily plain and spinster-like, and Bogart unnecessarily dirty and unkempt. She indicated her disapproval by saying things like "tch tch" or "oh, no." I thought, "This is the worst night of my life!" There were commercial interruptions, and I was dying to start talking about her reactions, but she suggested we wait until we had seen the entire movie and could talk without interruption.

ARI: And when it was over?

MARY ANN: The first thing she did was turn to me and say that she could see why I liked it. I was shocked. And I asked her why, because she had disliked so much about the movie. And then she began to give me her analysis of my positive response to the movie.

First, she asked me questions about my reactions to the characters of Bogart and Hepburn, and brought me to understand that I really didn't consider him a heroic type, that I had overlooked those naturalistic touches (the growling stomach, his crudeness, his dirty clothes), and that my positive response was to Hepburn. I admired a woman who didn't fold up and give up. In the story, she conceives of a plan to sink an enemy ship, and she is determined that they will do it together. And Ayn pointed this out to me: that I was responding to the *abstraction* of determination and heroism, and overlooking some of the unsavory concretes. It was selective awareness, on my part. I remember very clearly one thing she said: that this is an example of someone seeing past the bad directorial touches in the movie, seeing past the things that undercut the characters of both Hepburn and Bogart.

She was sympathetic about my desire to see something heroic in human behavior, but she pointed out what I had failed to see in the movie – or, more exactly, the aspects I dismissed or glossed over in my appraisal and, consequently, in my response.

ARI: So, it stopped being one of your favorites?

MARY ANN: No, not ever. But, once I saw and understood the things she was pointing out, I liked it less as a *total* movie.

ARI: Did you feel you had lost a value?

MARY ANN: I think I did feel that, in the beginning. But it was not because she encouraged me to give it up. There was never any suggestion of that. She was teaching me how to discriminate, how to introspect and understand *which* aspects of something I responded to. She was encouraging me to try to seek out the reasons for that response. And, of course, it applied to more than one's response to a movie.

ARI: How did you feel when you saw it again?

MARY ANN: It was a long time before I saw it again – in those days, there weren't any VCRs or videos to rent, and one had to wait until it came back on TV or to a movie theatre. And when I did see it again, I was much more perceptive about the negative aspects of the movie. But, my response to the *abstraction* – what I responded to initially – hasn't changed.

ARI: Tell me about another discussion.

MARY ANN: There was one about a painting I discovered in college. It's by Cézanne. It's very simple – it shows a road next to a high wall, and there are tall trees along the road. The first time I saw a picture of it, I liked it immediately. I was curious to hear her reaction. I knew that she didn't like Cézanne; I didn't either, not the total of his work. But this painting was an exception for me. And I couldn't put my finger on why my response to it was so strong. One evening, I took over a slide of it and a projector, showed her the painting, and asked her what she thought about it.

ARI: Why were her response and her thoughts important to you?

MARY ANN: Because when I like something, it's an added pleasure to know that my friends like it, too. But, also, I knew that I was going to learn something. I didn't know what, but there never was a discussion with her when I didn't learn something.

ARI: And what happened?

MARY ANN: She asked me if I could tell her why I liked it. I don't remember all that I said. I recall talking about two things: the secluded, peaceful setting, and the sharp contrast between sunlight and shade in the painting – what she called "stylized sunlight." She said she could understand why I was responding to that aspect of it.

ARI: What did you learn?

MARY ANN: It was another example of that same approach she used with *The African Queen*: try to identify why you like something, and in which respect. Do you like the total? Which aspects appeal to you? What do they mean to you, personally? Ask yourself, is what you like really in the painting, or are you bringing something to it and responding to that?

ARI: Did you learn why you liked it?

MARY ANN: No, not in every respect. I agreed with her analysis of the sunlight and shade, and I did find that attractive. But there was something else I couldn't name. When I told her this, she suggested that perhaps I was responding to something I was bringing to the painting, something that was triggered by an aspect of the work. I asked her how I could get at this "something" – whatever it was. And then she suggested that I begin by compiling a list of other art works I liked, and then ask myself if they had anything in common. That was the beginning of an odyssey for me that lasted a few years and took me all the way back to early childhood. Finally, I did understand why I loved the painting.

The value of that discussion was her stress on the importance of understanding the reasons behind artistic preferences. Doing so puts you in touch with yourself, and you identify your basic values in the process.

ARI: Did she like the painting?

MARY ANN: She was lukewarm. She liked the strong contrast between sunlight and shade, but she didn't like the loose, sketchy style. However, in the discussion, she was focused on my responses and the reasons for them, not on hers.

ARI: I heard that you played some of your favorite Frank Sinatra recordings for her.

MARY ANN: This was the spring of 1980, after her husband died.[1] On one visit, I took all my favorite Sinatras to play for her, and so did Sue Ludel,[2] who was also a Sinatra fan. It was Sue's idea. Ayn agreed to listen to them and comment.

ARI: Did she like any of them?

MARY ANN: She liked one very much, "Winners" – especially the lyrics; lines like "Here's to the battle, whatever it's for, to ask the best of ourselves, and give much more." She didn't like the

---

[1] Frank O'Connor died in Manhattan on November 7, 1979.
[2] Sue Ludel, then married to Leonard Peikoff

swing arrangement of "I've Got You Under My Skin." She said that the tempo destroyed the song, which had been written with a Latin beat. I remember verbatim her comment about one of my favorites, "Here's That Rainy Day." She said, disapprovingly, "Mary Ann, it has *no* melody!" I could see her point, but that didn't change my mind about it. She asked me why I liked it. I said that the arrangement featured the purity of his voice and the clarity of every word he sang. And then she made some very perceptive and positive comments about his phrasing, his enunciation, the way he used his voice to convey the emotional quality of a song. She was not a Sinatra fan and hadn't listened to his music over the years. But, when she did, she grasped what was unique about him.

ARI: Did she enjoy the session?

MARY ANN: For a while. But after about an hour of it, we had to stop. She said it was giving her a headache! Sue had brought over some gay operetta marches to play as an antidote. They cured the headache.

CONVERSATIONS WITH CHARLES

ARI: Charles, let's turn to your discussions with Miss Rand.

CHARLES: One that comes to mind is a discussion about white lies. It took place in the early morning hours of that January 1, with the four of us – Ayn, Frank, Mary Ann, and me – sitting around the dining room table.

ARI: Who raised it?

CHARLES: I did. I thought white lies were bad, but I couldn't make a full argument against them. Ayn proceeded to explain. But, first, let me say that I raised the subject on the spur of the moment, thinking that she would reserve a full discussion for a later time. However, she launched right in.

ARI: What did she say?

CHARLES: First she said that a white lie is understood to be a harmless fib told with good motives, usually to protect the listener from bad news. But, she said emphatically, it is not harmless; it is insidious. A white lie is worse than a straight-out lie because not only is the element of faking reality present, but the person to whom you are telling the lie is thereby deemed by you incapable of facing reality and needs protection from it. That is, the person is deemed insufficiently rational to accept a fact of reality and deal with it.

The example she gave was of the husband who has to have minor surgery and wants to spare his wife the worry. So, instead of telling her the truth, that he is going to the hospital as an outpatient, he tells her he is going to play golf. That is the epitome of a white lie. After his treatment is over and he is fine, he tells his wife about the surgery. A wife who has any self-respect is justifiably furious when she finds out the truth. She is angry that he considered her insufficiently stable to face up to whatever the present and the future might hold. Ayn said that a terrible consequence of his action is the undermining of her confidence in him to be a truthful partner.

ARI: Did she elaborate?

CHARLES: Yes. She said it puts the wife in the position of not knowing when he is being truthful and when he is shielding her from the facts of reality. This will lead to estrangement and distrust.

ARI: Did she say how this situation can be rectified?

CHARLES: First, by the husband fully understanding the meaning of his action – what it says about him and his evaluation of his wife. He has to be convinced why it is wrong to tell white lies, and this will take some rethinking on his part. The wife has to know that he fully understands the issue and more – how his white lie has affected her. Then, he has to pledge never to do it again, and live up to it.

She explained another possible outcome of the situation. Suppose, she said, something did go wrong during the surgery and the husband died. Not only is the wife left to deal with the catastrophe, but she is also left to wonder, forever, why he was not truthful with her about the incident. And worse, she will wonder how many other times he wasn't truthful. No matter how deep her love for him, her memory of him will always be marred by these doubts. She will feel let down in a fundamental way.

Ayn added that she did not mean to imply, by using the husband as an example, that wives don't make the same mistake. But, more often, the husband sees himself in the role of protector and may be motivated to shield his spouse with a white lie.

In a proper marriage, she said, the wife (or husband) will want to know what difficulty has to be dealt with, and how best to deal with it. She will want to be there to aid and comfort her husband. A marriage, Ayn said, is a partnership, an equal partnership. And the vows about "in sickness and in health" are not idle words divorced from meaning or application.

As to the wife who wants to be protected with white lies, who wants her husband to build a buffer between her and reality – Ayn called her "an irresponsible child" and an "evader."

ARI: How was she during a discussion? Did she tend to dominate, because of her knowledge?

CHARLES: Dominate? Only in the sense that she usually had more to say than anyone else. She would not push or pull or pressure you. She would be quiet while you thought, and quiet while you spoke. She did not interrupt your thoughts. She let you speak it out, even though she was pretty sure where you were going. She let you take all the steps you needed to make your point. You had a sense that whatever you said, you were understood, that you were being listened to. If she saw that you were making a mistake in your reasoning, she let you make that mistake. Then she analyzed the mistake at length, and she showed you what incorrect premises led you to the incorrect conclusion. In almost every discussion, there were two parts: the subject under consideration, and how my mind was working.

ARI: You mean, "Check your premises"?

CHARLES: Yes, that was part of it. If you had a problem checking them, she helped you along.

ARI: Can you speak about another discussion?

CHARLES: There was one about surprise parties and what was wrong with them.

ARI: You raised this question?

CHARLES: Yes. Mary Ann mentioned to me that the Collective had given Ayn a surprise dinner party to celebrate the publication of *Atlas Shrugged*, and that Ayn was very annoyed and did not enjoy the party. Like most people, I grew up accepting surprise parties as fun events, and I was curious about Ayn's attitude. So I brought it up one evening when we were there. Mary

Ann had had a discussion with her on the issue some years earlier.

ARI: Miss Rand didn't suggest that you ask Mary Ann?

CHARLES: No, that was not her policy. If a question was asked of her, she was the one to answer it. And she always held my context when explaining something to me.

ARI: What do you mean?

CHARLES: Ayn understood that not everyone integrates knowledge in the same way and at the same rate, and she let my way and rate of understanding the issue be her guide. This put me at mental ease. I knew that there wouldn't be any tension about keeping up with her. When Ayn explained an issue, she was explaining it to *someone*.

ARI: What were her objections to surprise parties?

CHARLES: I can give you a summary of what she said, not the progression. She had several objections. First and foremost is that it puts the recipient in the position of having to suddenly switch his context and deal with an unplanned for, unexpected situation. What, she asked, is the value in that? This is what we do in cases of emergency, she said. We shouldn't be put in the position of doing it for a celebration. She objected to being "put in a position" by someone else, of being deprived of choice in the matter.

The giver mistakenly thinks that the shock of the surprise will be more appreciated than a planned-for party. On the contrary, she said. The recipient gets no benefit whatever from the surprise element. It adds no value over and above what would be derived from a planned-for occasion. Instead, it detracts from the value of the occasion, because the recipient is put in the position of being a guest of honor and a host at the same time. He has to put his shock aside and greet people he had not expected to see (or perhaps not wanted to see), he is expected to be grateful to the party givers who study him for his reactions, he is expected to be gracious and charming when he may feel annoyance, or anger, or overwhelmed by the situation.

ARI: Did she say anything about the motives of the surprise party giver?

CHARLES: She said that the motives were bad if the party giver deliberately made it a surprise affair because he knew the recipient would refuse a party if offered. If the recipient doesn't want a party, then there shouldn't be a party.

She made additional points. The giver has no right to be the final unilateral authority on how anyone's achievement is to be celebrated. And the giver has no right to be the sole arbiter to determine who the guests are. Most important, the giver has no right to be the one who determines how any evening out of the life of the recipient is to be spent. That's up to the recipient.

Added to all this is that the recipient is deprived of the pleasure of anticipation, which adds greatly to the enjoyment of the celebration.

ARI: But some people enjoy surprise parties, don't they?

CHARLES: That may be. She couldn't see any valid reason for them. But that's something the giver should find out in advance, if the pleasure of the recipient is the first consideration. And, she said, it should be.

HUMOR

ARI: Can you give some examples of lighter moments?

MARY ANN: Sure. In the late fifties, one afternoon Frank and I went to see *Lust for Life*, the Vincent Van Gogh movie with Kirk Douglas. And, of course, it included the gory episode of Van Gogh mutilating his ear. When we returned home, Ayn wanted to hear about the movie and especially about Frank's response. "How was it?" she asked. And Frank said, with a smile, "Well, lend me your ear." And she said, laughing irresistibly, some words to the effect that it was a gruesome remark. But she couldn't stop laughing.

ARI: She liked his sense of humor?

MARY ANN: She loved his wit. Some of it's in her novels. His humor was in the form of spontaneous comments, tailored to the situation. Here's an instance of it: from time to time, Charles and I would call from Maryland just to say hello and see how they were doing. During the years when Ayn and Charles were stamp collecting, the conversation would always turn to stamps, and while they talked about stamps, Frank and I remained on the line as silent listeners. One time, Ayn and Charles talked for about twenty minutes. Finally, Ayn said, "Frank, are you and Mary Ann still on?" His response: "Oh, yes. But, we're a little older."

ARI: Did Miss Rand ever tell unphilosophical jokes?

CHARLES: Not to me. But she did tell a very funny story about a man in his hotel room, calling down to the desk to complain about his bags not being sent up. I remember only one line of a long monologue, all of which Ayn had memorized verbatim: "It's damn seldom what happens to my luggage around here!" And she liked Professor Irwin Corey, the character on television who was advertised as the "world's foremost authority." He was the pretentious, befuddled professor-type, in words and in appearance. He would speak nonsense with great pomposity, such as his admonition, "We must circumvent the periphery!" That always tickled her.

MARY ANN: One night, Ayn, Frank, and I were discussing the difficulties of adults learning to speak a foreign language. I said to her, "I can teach you to speak American Indian in a minute." And she answered immediately, with a note of challenge in her voice, "How?" I said nothing, I just looked at her and smiled. Frank got it right away and broke up. Then she caught on, laughing in a protesting sort of way. She was interested in the fact that Frank got it immediately, while it took her longer. She commented on the difference in the way each grew up. Humor was never a part of her upbringing; the atmosphere in her home was more formal. But Frank was typically American in his response to humor. She asked me for another example to see if he got it before she did.

ARI: What was it?

MARY ANN: More pseudo-Indian talk. I asked them to repeat after me, "O wah, tah nah, siam." And to keep repeating it until they got it.

ARI: O wah, tah nah, siam?

MARY ANN: Yes. After a few repeats, Frank got it and bent over laughing. She had to do it a few more times; she did it in her head and out loud, and then she finally got it. She wanted to know where I learned it, and I explained that it was something I learned in childhood, something to get bullies and mean playmates to repeat. She said she would have to use it the next time she had a conversation with someone impervious to a rational argument!

CHARLES: One of her cats was an attractive mongrel which she named "Ali," and which I took to be an allusion to Muhammad Ali, the prizefighter whom she admired because he was proud of his ability and made a point of saying so. That may well have been the case, but it was also a joke. I didn't get it until she said, "Ali cat."

And there is Frank's classic comment on the Rockettes, the precision dancers at Radio City Music Hall: "If you've seen one, you've seen 'em all."

Chapter IV

The Celebrity

THE CELEBRITY

ARI: Let's turn to Ayn Rand the celebrity and her attitude toward fans.

MARY ANN: She *was* a celebrity, but she didn't act like one.

ARI: How do you mean?

MARY ANN: She didn't want or need an adoring, protective entourage around her, going with her everywhere she went, fawning over her, flattering her. She frowned on that practice. She had seen a lot of that in Hollywood and considered it phony.

CHARLES: There was an appealing reserve to her. She was gracious about the attention paid to her by fans and the applause she generated at public appearances. But she didn't go out of her way to call attention to herself.

ARI: Can you give some recollections of Ayn Rand, the public figure?

CHARLES: Whenever she came to Washington, D.C., to answer questions after a lecture had been given on her philosophy, as many as 500 people attended. Here's what happened the first time she came: when the lecture was over, she was announced, and she entered from the back of the lecture hall. In order to reach the podium, she had to walk up a rather long center aisle, right through the audience. The minute she entered, there was a crash of applause, and it followed her all the way; people craned their necks to see her; some stood on their chairs for a better look. It was a wonderful response, and she appreciated it – and said so to the audience. But after the question period was over, she took us aside and said that she did not enjoy that long walk. She felt self-conscious, and said it had the aura of the emperor entering the audience hall. She requested that next time she enter through a side entrance. We did that for her next appearance, and she was much happier with the arrangement. She was not seeking adulation.

ARI: Was she recognized on the street or other places?

MARY ANN: Only once, in my experience. Writers are not as famous as movie stars; her face wasn't in the news constantly. But she knew she would be photographed by tourists. She didn't like it.

ARI: Why?

MARY ANN: In part, vanity. She was not photogenic. She didn't want unflattering snapshots of her floating around. And she resented the intrusion into her privacy.

ARI: What about the time she was recognized?

MARY ANN: That was in a neighborhood restaurant, near her apartment. It wasn't a place frequented by celebrities. Ayn, Leonard, Sue, Charles, and I were having lunch. I looked up to see a man pointing a camera at her, and immediately raised my hand to block the shot, and so did Sue. The tourist was surprised. Ayn explained to him that she did not like to be photographed without her permission. He was a fan, and well-meaning, and their parting was cordial. Of course, at large gatherings, people took snapshots from afar. She couldn't stop that.

ARI: What about at lectures and other places where people expected to see her?

CHARLES: Always the gracious lady. We accompanied her to Ford Hall Forum in Boston a number of times. Her appearance always generated long lines of people waiting outside for admission to the lecture hall. It was a good walk from the street to the hall entrance, and people always recognized her as she approached. You could hear comments like "there she is" or "there's Ayn Rand," and people smiled and waved. And she always smiled and waved back. One time she was speaking to us and didn't notice them. I said, "They're waving at you," and she stopped in the middle of a thought to acknowledge them with a smile and a wave.

ARI: Did they rush up for autographs?

MARY ANN: No, they didn't want to lose their places in line! It was not unusual for people to wait for hours, sometimes in the rain. The Ford Hall lectures were given in the evening, and one of the Ford Hall officials told her that often the line started in the morning.

ARI: In a word, how did she treat the public and her fans?

MARY ANN: Respectfully. She took them seriously. I was a fan when I met her, and that's how she treated me.

If you want lots of evidence of this attitude, and of her benevolence, just read her answers to fan letters published in *Letters of Ayn Rand*.[1] In those letters, you see how much time she spent acknowledging their comments and answering their questions. There was nothing "form letter" about her responses. She answered *specific* questions with *specific* answers. If the writer's letter indicated some confusion and misunderstanding about an issue, she took the time to clarify the issue. Just look at the length of some of those letters, and the detailed answers she gave. And, of course, not just to fans, but to friends, acquaintances, relatives, professional associates. And on subjects ranging from technical philosophical issues to her fondness for cats. You can get an education from reading her letters.

ARI: What kind of fans did she want, did she ever say?

CHARLES: Intelligent readers seriously interested in ideas. That is all that mattered to her. She knew that not all fans understood the philosophy or took ideas as seriously as she would have liked. But she was a great one for giving people the benefit of the doubt.

She didn't need admiration from fans to boost her self-esteem, she didn't look to them for confirmation that her ideas were right or that she was a great writer. But she did appreciate the fans who wrote to express their admiration for her and her work.

---

[1] See Michael S. Berliner (ed.), *Letters of Ayn Rand*, Penguin Dutton, 1995.

In one of the letters, she writes that she feels "an interested affection" for people interested in ideas. And that names the attitude she projected when dealing with fans.

ARI: Any interesting anecdotes about her meeting up with fans?

MARY ANN: I remember one incident she told us about. This happened in the fifties, I think before *Atlas* was published, or soon after.

One afternoon, she took a cab to a business meeting uptown. When she was coming home, it was raining and it was rush hour, and she couldn't get a cab. So she decided to take the bus. As she was sitting down, she noticed that the woman in front of her had a paperback copy of *The Fountainhead*, an edition that had her picture on the back cover. Now, here's the charming, playful aspect of Ayn Rand. She tapped the woman on the shoulder, the woman turned around and said, "Yes?" and Ayn pointed to the paperback and told the woman to look on the back cover. When the woman realized that Ayn Rand was sitting behind her on the bus, she was very surprised and excited. She asked Ayn to autograph her book, which Ayn did. Then other people on the bus observed what was happening and inquired about the woman signing autographs, and this led to a few others requesting autographs. Ayn told this story with such delight, and said it was the best bus ride she had ever had.

ARI: Anything from later years?

CHARLES: This was more than an incident. It was an entire afternoon. In April 1977 Ford Hall Forum gave a luncheon in her honor, in recognition of the years she had spoken there and the support she had generated for the Forum. Invitations were sent out to the Forum's mailing list. The Forum was very surprised by the response – by the number who attended and the distances they came. There were hundreds at the luncheon, from all over the United States and many from foreign countries.

All attendees were seated at round tables in a very large room. There was a raised platform with a long table for the guest of honor and officials from the Forum. It was empty while the attendees were being seated. Then, when we were all assembled, an official from the Forum welcomed everyone, and said that he would announce the guests who were to be seated at the head table. And he asked us to hold our applause until all the guests were seated. Well, you can imagine that no one there was going to follow that instruction! So, he began to introduce the guests by name, and, one by one, they entered and stood at the table. The room was silent. Then, he announced "Miss Ayn Rand." She entered and walked up to the table. There was a burst of applause – it was deafening. Everyone stood up, clapping and cheering – there were a few whistles, too. She stood there, smiling broadly, eyes shining. Then, he announced "Frank O'Connor," and Frank walked in – again, the house broke into sustained applause. It was absolutely wonderful.

MARY ANN: It was announced that she would sign autographs after lunch. When that time came, people crowded around the table with copies of her books. At first, they were three and four deep around the table. So, to make the process faster and easier, a few of us had the guests form lines.

Frank stayed at the table with her, and people wanted his signature, too. Before he signed his name the first time, he practiced it on the tablecloth. One guest wanted the tablecloth! The process took over two hours. Many people had more than one book with them. And many didn't want to leave after receiving their autographs. They stood around, watching. They wanted to be in the room as long as she was in the room. It was tiring for her, but she was determined not to leave anyone out.

CHARLES: Then, we walked with Ayn and Frank to the elevator, and a contingent of people followed, at a respectful distance – and they waited until the elevator doors closed, waving goodbye, saying they would see her at the lecture that evening. She nodded enthusiastically, and waved back.

Here's another example of Ayn the celebrity: one night the O'Connors took Mary Ann and me to dinner at "21."[2] Ayn had been there before for business lunches and was known to some of the personnel. We were taken upstairs to be seated. There were tables in the center of the room where celebrities would be

---

[2] A famous Manhattan restaurant, frequented by celebrities

noticed if they were seated there; they would be the center of attention. Ayn requested that we be seated in a quiet area to the side, where we could have some privacy and talk. She never looked for the spotlight.

In the downstairs area, I had noticed some autographed books enclosed in a glass case, some six or seven of them, all from famous authors. I wrote to the restaurant manager telling him that we had been there as guests of Ayn Rand and asked if he would like to have an autographed copy of her novel *Atlas Shrugged*. He replied immediately that he would very much like to have it on display. I wrote to Ayn advising her of this and offering to supply the book, but she insisted on sending it herself.

ARI: She didn't mind your not asking her first?

CHARLES: Not at all. She liked the idea and said she was grateful to me for taking the initiative. Ayn did not take this kind of thing for granted. She didn't act like the all-important celebrity who accepted such gestures as her due. That was part of her charm. She was not a poseur. In fact, Ayn hated phoniness of any sort and if you were being phony or she thought you were being phony, she said so.

ARI: An example or two?

CHARLES: One night, she and I were playing Scrabble and she made a clever play involving six tiles, using a word I hadn't heard of. It was impressive. I exclaimed, "Good show!" She looked up at me and said somewhat mockingly, "I didn't know you were British." In using the phrase, I didn't think I was putting on airs. But from her perspective, it looked as if I were. It was typical of her not to let anything be passed over as if it didn't happen, however seemingly small.

Another example happened when we drove them to the White House in 1976 for a dinner given by President Ford honoring Malcolm Fraser, Prime Minister of Australia. When I stopped the car at the designated entrance, White House personnel came to open all four doors. They helped Ayn and Frank out of the car. I got out to say goodbye to them because I knew I wouldn't see them again before they left Washington. Usually I would give her a hug and a kiss, but I didn't want to disturb her hair or makeup, so I leaned over to kiss her hand. She didn't like it one bit; she whispered that it was too continental a gesture, especially in such an American setting. Whereupon she gave *me* a big hug and kiss.

ARI: Can you tell us more about this White House visit?

CHARLES: Dinner guests were instructed to drive to a specified gate; Ayn showed their invitations and we were told to drive through and follow a road to a side entrance. The drive took us across the White House grounds. Except for the Swiss Alps and Mont Blanc, I had never known her to be impressed by natural scenery. But the sight impressed her so that she asked me to slow down so we could all take it in. "Absolutely beautiful" is what she said about stately trees casting long shadows on broad, green, sloping lawns, about well-tended hedges and the touches of color in flower beds. She said it all looked as if nature had been carefully arranged. She commented that it was a marvelous introduction to the home.

ARI: Did she say anything about that evening?

CHARLES: She spoke about the elegance of the occasion. From the moment they entered the White House, there was an aide close by, so they were never left to stand and wonder what to do next. At the time, Shirley Temple Black was Chief of Protocol and she presented the guests in the receiving line to the President and the First Lady. When it came Ayn's turn, Shirley Temple exclaimed, "Oh, Miss Rand!" in an approving manner. Ayn said they were made to feel at home.

After dinner, guests were standing around and conversing with one another. Ayn felt a hand touch her shoulder, and a man's voice behind her said to please excuse him, he wanted to get by. She turned around, and was surprised to see that it was the President. There he was, she said, moving casually through his home, mingling with his guests. She liked the atmosphere of gracious informality. She added that she was glad their visits to the White House were during President Ford's administration.

ARI: So this wasn't her first visit to the White House?

CHARLES: No. She had met President Ford two years earlier, in 1974, when Alan Greenspan was sworn in as chairman of the Council of Economic Advisors. He had invited Ayn and Frank to attend the ceremony and had arranged for them to meet President Ford in the Oval Office. She was impressed with that occasion, too. When we met them afterward, the first thing she said was: "We met the President!" She didn't take it for granted.

MARY ANN: Getting back to the Malcolm Fraser dinner, after exiting the car and saying goodbye to us, Ayn and Frank were escorted to the doorway of the White House. They were happily excited but they didn't forget that we were there. At the entrance, they stopped and turned around to smile and wave at us. I'll always remember her wave – it was a quick movement of her hand, like a cross between a wave and a salute.

Chapter V

Ayn Rand on Negatives

AYN RAND ON NEGATIVES

ARI: I've heard that Miss Rand was not shy about expressing her evaluation in public of something that displeased her. Did either of you ever witness this?

MARY ANN: Along with a few friends, I attended a piano recital at Carnegie Hall with Ayn and Frank. The artist was Witold Malcuzynski, and the program was predominantly Romantic music. We were seated in the front row, directly beneath the pianist. At the end of each Romantic piece, Ayn expressed her approval by smiling broadly and holding her hands up as she applauded. Then, he played a modern piece; I don't remember what it was, but it was awful. At the end of that piece, some people in the audience stood up and applauded. Ayn – without taking her eyes off the pianist – remained seated. She raised her arms slowly, then lowered them and sat on her hands.

ARI: Did he see it?

MARY ANN: Oh, yes. I was watching him watch her. He saw her disapproval. She said later that sitting on one's hands was a common practice in Europe and that he would know what the gesture meant.

CHARLES: I had a similar experience, although in this case she was vocal. In the late seventies, Ayn, Frank, Sue, Leonard, Mary Ann, and I went to the Metropolitan Opera for a performance of Tchaikovsky's opera *Eugene Onegin*, an opera that Ayn knew and liked. She was seated between Frank and me, and seemed to be enjoying the performance. However, during the ballroom scene, she got very annoyed. I heard her take a deep breath, she nudged my arm and said, "Oh!" and words to the effect that it was terrible. She did the same with Frank. She expressed her disapproval loudly enough to be heard by those seated around us. When Frank and I whispered that she was disturbing people, she stopped. But she had made her point.

ARI: What did she object to?

CHARLES: The scene was romantic: the music was beautiful, the setting was elegant. Suddenly, members of the female chorus broke out into something like a can-can dance. They turned their backs to the audience, raised their filmy skirts, and pushed out their behinds and wiggled them at the audience. It was ugly and shockingly out of context – a deliberate undercutting of the romantic values of the scene. Ayn made her disapproval known. When the opera was over, she vowed never to go to the Metropolitan Opera again. She said that it had to have been done by conscious intention, a deliberate slap in the face at a Romantic work of art. She said she couldn't sit there and be silent, not when values were being attacked. That was a vintage Ayn Rand incident.

ARI: Is it true that she expressed disapproval during question periods after lectures?

MARY ANN: Yes, but her critics have made too much of those incidents, especially about their frequency in public; they've magnified it out of all proportion.

No one should forget that she defined a philosophy which has improved countless lives. She has inspired readers, by telling them that their minds are capable of understanding reality, and by giving them a morality of life. She has given them the incentive to achieve goals and move forward; she has created works of art in which man is an *exalted* being. Who else is doing that today in literature? Now, there were times when she did get angry in public, during question periods after a lecture. But to focus on those occasions is misleading. You have to ask: what is important about Ayn Rand? That she wrote *Atlas Shrugged* and defined a philosophy one can live by, or that, at times, she was capable of getting very angry? They are not equivalents.

ARI: You saw this anger yourself, during the question periods?

MARY ANN: Yes, but certainly not at every question period. And it's important to understand that she was not angry at anyone personally. She did not know the people involved; she was speaking to strangers. And many of the questions she answered were written questions – neither she nor the audience knew who had asked the questions; only the questioners knew. What's relevant here is that she expressed anger and indignation, not so much at the person asking a question but at the *ideas* expressed, or ideas she thought were implicit in the question asked. That was the focus of her anger.

ARI: Can one of you elaborate on this point?

CHARLES: Ayn was *perceptive*. She could see what assumptions were behind certain questions; she could detect the hidden agendas, the unnamed ideas. She knew when someone was, for example, really questioning the validity of reason or advocating altruism – without saying it openly. And she knew what those ideas would lead to if put into effect; she knew the *practical consequences* of those ideas. She understood that man's survival was at stake. Ayn was always the defender of man's life and values, and when she saw them being attacked, in any form, she responded forcefully. She was not a "tolerant" person. If what you said was evil or seriously wrong, she let you know it and she let you know what she thought and felt about it. (There were other reasons for her anger, as well – see Leonard Peikoff's memoir mentioned above.)

ARI: Were there any kinds of questions she especially disliked?

MARY ANN: She didn't like questions that began with: "Miss Rand, I understand what you said about so-and-so, but don't you think...?" – followed by the questioner presenting a different point of view. That form of the question implied that Ayn was saying one thing while thinking something else, that she was being hypocritical. Often her response was, "No, if I had thought so, I would have said so." It was said in a very matter-of-fact tone of voice. But sometimes she answered with anger. One night, I heard her explain to an audience just *why* that form of the question was offensive and improper, *what* it implied, and *why* she was indignant. Everyone benefited from hearing her analysis.

ARI: Can you give a specific example of when she responded angrily to a question?

MARY ANN: Someone asked her for her views on immigration, if she thought it was a good thing. And she got indignant immediately at the very idea that anyone might be opposed to immigration, that a country might not let immigrants in. One of the things she said in her answer was, "Where would I be today if America closed its doors to immigrants?" That really hit home; I'm sure everyone there realized that she would not have survived in Soviet Russia, that a person with her ideas would have died in prison, somewhere in Siberia. In her answer, she was defending people who were seeking freedom and a better life. And I think she was assuming that immigrants would be like she was — ready and able to make their own way, accepting help if voluntarily given by individuals but not expecting government handouts. But it was clear that she was angry at the *idea*, not at the person asking the question.

I heard people saying things like "I had no idea what I was really advocating." Ayn was teaching the students the importance of analyzing their ideas, of understanding what was implicit in what they had been taught to believe and why it was wrong and often evil.

CHARLES: I'd like to add two points here. One is that her expressions of anger were the exception, not the rule. Two, they were often followed by applause from the audience — because the listeners were inspired by hearing someone speaking up for and defending what was right and good. They had heard, over and over again, mealy-mouthed speakers afraid to take a position — or suggesting that there are always two sides to a question — or that nothing is black and white. To have been subjected to those attitudes from childhood on up, and then to hear Ayn Rand take a firm position and defend it with conviction – this was a cause for cheering. The audience response was not only to the content of her ideas, but to her manner of expressing them. She was medicine for the soul.

MARY ANN: All those adults who taught us never to get angry, or if we did, not to express it, to hide our emotions when we were offended or felt we were being treated unjustly, to remain calm, to maintain an even keel, for God's sake, don't blow up, no matter what – these people didn't do us any favors by urging us to suppress, to live like glazed, non-reacting creatures.

ARI: Did she ever get angry during philosophical discussions when people were slow to get her point?

MARY ANN: I wouldn't call the response "anger" – it was more exasperation bordering on impatience. The best example of this I can remember was a group discussion, before *Atlas* was published. Some of the Collective, myself included, were having difficulty demonstrating that life is the standard of morality. So, the issue was explained again, and we were asked to write an essay on the subject and bring it back the following Saturday night. A few of us did, and she was surprised to learn that only Leonard was able to do it correctly. The rest of us made errors or left out steps in the argument. I remember her looking puzzled by it, for the issue had been discussed in detail and we had all read that section of Galt's speech over and over. But she did get very annoyed when someone, I think Nathan, suggested that maybe that section needed more explication.

ARI: What did she say?

MARY ANN: She said that she couldn't make that section of the speech any clearer than she had. But what really interested her was how our minds were working, how we were processing the information, what we were doing mentally, what we were doing right and what we were doing wrong in our thinking.

I've never forgotten that evening, because it opened up a subject new to me – introspecting to analyze one's thinking processes. I had the same experience with her some years later when I was revising my lectures on esthetics. I hadn't given sufficient thought to a certain issue of style, and I couldn't explain my reasons for introducing it in the way I did. I could see her growing impatience, and I remember clearly her frowning and saying, "What's happened to your epistemology, Mary Ann?" So, we spent the rest of the evening discussing that. She wanted to get at the reasons for my muddled thinking, to identify why, as she put it, my mental wires were crossed. That was typically Ayn. If she saw you floundering and having difficulty thinking clearly, she wanted to help you, to get you back on track.

ARI: Any final thoughts on the subject?

CHARLES: Just this: her expressions of anger were not the outbursts of someone run by wild and uncontrolled emotions. She didn't use anger to intimidate people, as bullies do. When she got angry, it was precisely because she was a *thinker and an evaluator who was certain of her convictions.* She judged something as right or wrong, good or evil – and she responded accordingly. She didn't simmer and stew; she came to an immediate boil. Her thinking was not hampered and slowed down by chronic doubt, and her emotions were not suppressed or muted by it, either. Moreover, her emotions never clouded or distorted her thinking. And the anger didn't last. It was over almost as soon as it began.

MARY ANN: At some point, you are going to ask me what I miss about her. One of the things I miss most is what we've been talking about – her anger and righteous indignation, and what it came from. I miss knowing that there is someone in the world who always speaks out, unequivocally, against irrationality and injustice, and who not only denounces evil but *who defends the good.* She was mankind's intellectual guardian, a soldier in the battle of ideas. Her banner was always flying high.

When she died, someone made the following comment: now anger has gone out of the world. And I thought, it's true, and it's the world's loss, and mine.

CHARLES: And mine.

Chapter VI

Mr. and Mrs. Frank O'Connor

MR. AND MRS. FRANK O'CONNOR

ARI: Knowing the O'Connors for as long as you did and spending so much time with them, what impressed you about their relationship?

CHARLES: Ayn's Introduction to the 25th Anniversary Edition of *The Fountainhead* says it all. It was written in May 1968. I don't want to dilute the strength of her statements by paraphrasing them, so let me read some excerpts:

"…it would be impossible for me to discuss *The Fountainhead* without mentioning the man who made it possible for me to write it: my husband, Frank O'Connor.

"In a play I wrote in my early thirties, *Ideal*, the heroine, a screen star, speaks for me when she says: 'I want to see, real, living, and in the hours of my own days, that glory I create as an illusion. I want it real. I want to know that there is someone, somewhere, who wants it, too. Or else what is the use of seeing it, and working, and burning oneself for an impossible vision? A spirit, too, needs fuel. It can run dry.'

"Frank was the fuel. He gave me, in the hours of my own days, the reality of that sense of life which created *The Fountainhead* and he helped me to maintain it over a long span of years when there was nothing around us but a gray desert of people and events that evoked nothing but contempt and revulsion. The essence of the bond between us is the fact that neither of us has

Photo courtesy of the Estate of Ayn Rand

Frank O'Connor
1966

ever wanted or been tempted to settle for anything less than the world presented in *The Fountainhead*. We never will."

Ayn also writes in the Introduction about an evening when she felt profound discouragement about "things as they are." She says, "…it seemed as if I would never regain the energy to move one step farther toward 'things as they ought to be.' Frank talked to me for hours, that night. He convinced me of why one cannot give up the world to those one despises. By the time he finished, my discouragement was gone; it never came back in so intense a form."

That night, she told him she would dedicate *The Fountainhead* to him "because he had saved it."

What does this say about their relationship? This is a tribute written by a woman who is deeply in love with her husband, and about a husband who is deeply in love with his wife. You see, Frank understood Ayn. He knew what she valued, he knew what to say to help her restore her view of life and give her the motivation – the fuel – to move forward. And he didn't give up; he spoke for hours until he convinced her. And equally important, she respected his understanding of her – she knew she could turn to him for that encouragement. Is there anything more important in a marriage than understanding each other's values and encouraging each other to pursue them; than helping each other maintain that basic outlook on life that they hold in common? I don't think so. They were a devoted couple until the end of their days.

ARI: What signs of that did you observe in their daily life?

CHARLES: There were so many signs. For one thing, they were demonstrative about their affection. When they sat together or walked down the street together, they held hands. They kissed "hello" and "goodbye." Whenever Ayn and I were out at an all-day stamp show, she always wondered aloud what Frank was doing. She always called him her "top value." He was a constant in her life, in her awareness. Let me tell you about an incident that exemplifies this.

ARI: What is that?

CHARLES: I've spoken about the birthday party Mary Ann gave me when I turned fifty. She made me and my interests the theme of the party. The paper plates, cups, and napkins were red, white, and blue, which related to my patriotism. She designed a fifty-cent red, white, and blue stamp to commemorate the date, naming it "Charles Sures Semicentennial Celebration, 1922–1972." In fact, she designed a companion stamp, one with errors in the printing – everything in red was printed upside down! An artist drew them on cardboard and they were placed over two birthday cakes. Mary Ann had ordered food that I especially enjoyed. And the group birthday gift was the stamps Ayn had selected. The point of all this is that during the evening, Ayn turned to me and said that she envied Mary Ann because Mary Ann was having the pleasure of making me, her husband, the center, the focus of the evening in a very personal way. Ayn said she was inspired to do something like that for Frank.

MARY ANN: And the same was true of Frank: Ayn was always a focus in his life. If we were roaming through a department store, he would point out items of women's apparel and comment: "That would look good on Ayn." Or, "Ayn loves that color." Or, "I wonder if Ayn could use that scarf." In a museum he would comment about a painting: "I have to bring Ayn to see that." If we were coming back from an outing later than we had anticipated, he knew Ayn would worry, and so he called her to say we would be late.

In 1956, at Christmas time, when Ayn was nearing the end of the writing of *Atlas Shrugged*, Frank commented on how hard she had been working and said he needed to do something special for her. He wanted to buy her some luxury items and asked me where he could find beautiful and unusual lingerie. I told him about a shop on Fifth Avenue and 59th Street, which specialized in handmade items in fine silk and satin. He visited it and bought several lovely things for her.

And Ayn always wanted Frank near her. At functions like the Ford Hall Forum, at the conclusion of the evening she wanted Frank to be by her side while she was saying goodnight to the officials. He was her protector, physically and spiritually.

When Ayn was hospitalized for lung surgery, I stayed with Frank. He said it was important to keep up her spirits.

ARI: How did he do that?

MARY ANN: First, by visiting daily. We went in the afternoon, and made it a point to get there at approximately the same time each day. He wanted Ayn to know when to expect us. And he always looked marvelous – impeccably groomed in a suit, usually a white shirt, and a specially selected tie. He always wore ties with cheerful, bright colors – or with amusing designs. There was one she especially liked – it had kittens in the pattern. She never failed to notice his ties. She knew he was wearing them to add a cheerful touch to the rather drab room.

ARI: What did they talk about?

MARY ANN: She wanted to know what we had done during the day, if we had taken a walk, what we had seen, what we had for lunch, what we would have for dinner. She wanted all the details. She said that hearing them helped her to restore the context of normal living. He sat by the bed and they held hands. And when he went to sit by the window to watch the lights come on in buildings and on bridges, she didn't take her eyes off of him. She whispered to me that she loved looking at his profile framed by the window.

A major example of her devotion was her interest in his painting and the way she encouraged him in that venture.

ARI: Let's talk about that. Was he painting when you met him in 1954?

MARY ANN: No, he was working with a florist, and doing floral arrangements for lobbies of buildings. He had a business card billing him as "Francisco, the Lobbyist." That's an example of his sense of humor. I don't think it was full-time work.

ARI: How did he get into painting?

MARY ANN: It all began in the mid-fifties. During a Collective discussion about art and talent, Joan said that artistic talent was not innate, that anyone could learn to draw, given an interest and the incentive to learn. To illustrate her point, she offered to give lessons. A few of us joined the class, including Frank. Of everyone there, he was the only one who showed any promise or serious interest in art.

ARI: What were the signs of that?

MARY ANN: From the very beginning, Frank's drawing showed a developed sense of style. He had an individual way of doing things – whether he was drawing an egg or a human face. You could always tell if something was drawn by Frank. His work was bold; it had a quality of self-assurance, in spite of the flaws of a beginner. When the class ended, for Frank it was the beginning of a career.

ARI: How did his interest develop?

MARY ANN: He kept up his drawing, on his own. And he began to work on cityscapes in pastel. They were his first finished works in color, and they showed his inventiveness and love of dramatic and unusual arrangements.

ARI: Did he talk to you about his goals as an artist?

MARY ANN: Not very often. But here's an example of how he approached art. One summer, some of the Collective spent a day in the country. Frank and I took a stroll, and we saw a number of people sketching the scenery; they were all facing the same view of the countryside. It looked like a class of some sort. Frank volunteered that that was not his way of coming at things. He wanted to *invent* his scenes.

In that discussion, he did agree that one could learn by sketching from nature, and he wasn't opposed to that. He did a few sketches of rocks and trees that day. But he was opposed to having his subjects ready-made. He didn't want to paint the given in nature or anything else. He wanted his art to come from his imagination. He wanted to select and arrange his subject in his own way.

ARI: But he did go to art school?

MARY ANN: Yes, and that's where Ayn was involved. She encouraged him to seek instruction in art, so that he could develop his talent. She said his talent was too great to be left without professional guidance. She suggested that he might prefer private instruction to that of a school, if he could find a suitable teacher. Frank agreed, and one Saturday he and I visited art galleries, looking for an artist whose work he admired and who might give him private lessons. That wasn't successful. Ayn then asked me to help Frank investigate art schools. I had catalogs and brochures sent to him from about ten schools. Ayn studied them with Frank. He selected the Art Students League, which had an excellent reputation, fine instructors, and good facilities.

ARI: Did he enjoy being a student?

MARY ANN: Very much. Frank was a serious, dedicated, and conscientious student. He attended regularly, taking courses in life drawing and painting, anatomy, composition. When he wasn't studying at the League, he was working at home. Robert Brackman, a well-known painter, was one of his teachers. He told Ayn that Frank was an unusual student in the sense of coming to painting with fully developed ideas of what he wanted to accomplish.

Frank knew the end he wanted to achieve; he had to learn the means, he had to learn technique. That's what he got from the Art Students League.

ARI: How did Miss Rand react to this new direction in his life?

MARY ANN: Oh, she was so happy and so very proud of him. I was there a few times when he brought work home, such as an unfinished painting. He would explain to her how he reached that stage of the painting and what the next stage would be. I saw her listening intently. She would break into a smile and comment on how marvelously Frank was doing.

Privately, she said Frank's pursuit of this career was important to her because he was giving visual expression to what she called his "exalted sense of life." She said that after they left California and the ranch he managed, Frank didn't find a vocation or work in New York that was a full-time, all-consuming endeavor. But with painting, he was a man totally involved and totally committed, and he was thoroughly enjoying himself. Ayn continued to encourage him to expand his technical knowledge.

ARI: Anything in particular?

MARY ANN: She saw that he was having trouble with perspective. She knew that it was an important discipline for an artist, and encouraged him to increase his knowledge, to add to what he learned at the League by studying on his own. She knew that not having a firm grounding in perspective would hold him back. That no matter how creative his ideas for a painting might be, he needed technical knowledge to give expression to those ideas. She asked me to locate a good book on perspective. She thought that an older book, one written earlier in the century, would have better explanations and examples than the more recently written works. I did find one or two older books. I know that Ayn and Frank went over them together. She took his career seriously.

ARI: Did you ever watch him paint? What was he like?

MARY ANN: I sat for Frank a number of times. When he was at the easel, his concentration was total. It was as if the universe were narrowed down to a few elements: Frank, easel, palette, brushes, model. As if nothing else existed or mattered. He was completely absorbed. He even forgot to give me breaks during the afternoon. I or Ayn had to remind him.

ARI: Miss Rand came in when he was working?

MARY ANN: When he was painting in their apartment living room, she visited regularly. Once she came in, not just to see the progress of the painting, but to watch him at work. He was unaware of her; she watched for a few minutes, smiled at me, and then left. Later, she said, "Did you see the look on his face?" She said it was beautiful – the face of a man self-confidently in focus.

A few times, she offered advice about a painting in progress. This was a source of a little bit of friction between them.

ARI: Tell me about that.

MARY ANN: Frank painted in a style which Ayn personally liked – a style of clarity and precision, but not one of dry details. She would say things like "Make that edge a little sharper, darling," or

"The colors are running together," or "It's a little blurry in this part." Now, Ayn was very enthusiastic about what Frank was doing, and I don't think she made these comments as criticisms. She was calling things to his attention, things she thought he would want to be aware of. He listened, but didn't say anything. She would return to her desk, and he would resume painting. Once he said to me, "If she wants to paint, let her get her own canvas and paints and do it her way." This was followed by some of Frank's good-natured laughter.

The point is that Frank was as independent about his painting as he was about everything else. He had definite ideas, he knew what he wanted to achieve, and he proceeded to do it his way. He allowed nothing to get in his way. If, after her suggestions, he did make a change, it was because he thought it was right, not because she had suggested it. And I know that she admired that aspect of him – his independence and self-assertiveness as an artist. Once she said, approvingly, "He is a tiger at the easel." And Frank's response, good-natured as always, was, "Well, just don't grab me by the tail."

ARI: Did they ever quarrel?

CHARLES: I never witnessed a quarrel between them. This is not to say they didn't quarrel in private. But as I said earlier, they respected their privacy. One of the things they didn't do was quarrel and bicker in public. They had some very nice, old-fashioned civil ways of behavior.

MARY ANN: I came in once during what appeared to be a mild quarrel, and they stopped immediately. It was none of my business – I knew it and they knew it, too.

ARI: Did you ever see Miss Rand cry?

CHARLES: Twice, in all the years I knew her. Once, when one of her cats had died. We visited her a few days later, and when she told us about it her eyes brimmed with tears. The other time was at Frank's grave, which we visited with her in the spring following his death. She and Mary Ann hugged each other and had a few tears.

ARI: Do you have anything to add here?

MARY ANN: She cried briefly as we left the funeral home. In this context, I want to tell you about a beautiful thing Frank said about Ayn once. One evening, the three of us were talking about Ayn's first days in this country. I said I had heard that when her ship reached the pier, tears ran down her face as she looked up to the skyline of New York. I asked what those tears were for. Frank answered, "They were tears of splendor." And Ayn nodded in agreement.

CHARLES: I can add a sequel to our visit to Frank's grave, which shows Ayn's benevolence. We took a train home from the cemetery (the car I had rented broke down). I sat by the window, dozing off; Mary Ann was next to me and Ayn was sitting across the aisle from her. It had been a tiring, bittersweet trip. None of us felt like talking. As we approached New York City, the train entered the underground tunnels. Suddenly, both Ayn and Mary Ann stood up and I heard Mary Ann say, "Ayn, it's just what you described in *Atlas*." They were watching the tunnels and train tracks going off in a number of directions, and the red and green lights in semi-darkness suspended over the tracks. I watched, too. Ayn was grinning at the sight. It all lasted less than a minute, but we all felt different after it. We felt energized and eager. And Ayn did not let the episode pass without identifying what had happened. She said, "Our world has been restored."

Chapter VII

Personal Favorites

PERSONAL FAVORITES

ARI: Did she have any favorite foods?

MARY ANN: Ayn had a sweet tooth. She loved milk chocolate, fudge, and Godiva chocolates.

ARI: Any stories connected with them?

MARY ANN: Five-and-dime stores with candy counters sold chunks of milk chocolate. I said earlier that she didn't like to ask for favors, but chocolate was the exception. When I was living in New York, more than once she asked me to bring her some chocolate if I were near a dime store. She insisted on paying, of course. She enjoyed it as dessert, with black coffee.

ARI: What about the fudge?

CHARLES: There was a delicious fudge we used to bring her from Washington. It was made by hand, in small batches, by a local woman, and sold only at Garfinckel's, a D.C. department store. As an indication of how much she liked it, she once said, jokingly, "I would sell my soul for that fudge!"

MARY ANN: There's an amusing story connected with fudge, and it's an example of her sense of humor. Leonard was fond of the fudge, too. One year, I sent him two pounds, each pound in a separate box – one with her name, one with his. I expected him to deliver a box to her. Well, apparently, he didn't see the labels. And when he called to thank us, he thanked us for both

Photo courtesy of the Estate of Ayn Rand

Ayn Rand and Thunderbird
1964

pounds. But, by the time he called, most of the fudge had been eaten by Leonard and some friends. So, I phoned her to report the mishap and to say that I would send her another box. She said something like "Do you mean to tell me that he ate *both* boxes?" She sounded surprised and somewhat indignant. I said, jokingly, "Ayn, it's not as if he had just challenged the validity of the Law of Identity!" There was a pause, and then she answered, "Well, it's not that bad. *But it's close.*"

CHARLES: Ayn discouraged gift giving. However, not once did she ever refuse the fudge or discourage us from giving it to her. Of course, we got around the gift-giving restriction by offering it as a "non-gift." We stayed over at the O'Connors' a number of times when we visited New York, and the fudge was a gift to the hostess. She said she would accept it as a "non-hostess."

ARI: And did you bring her Godiva chocolates?

MARY ANN: No, that was never necessary. She kept herself fully supplied with Godivas! B. Altman had a Godiva counter which she visited. She enjoyed everything about them – the chocolates, of course, but also the lovely gold boxes they came in, and the neat, little compartments inside the boxes. She saved the boxes, using them for storage of small personal things, like costume jewelry which fit nicely into the compartments. And once, she cut out Christmas crowns from the gold boxes for Oscar and Oswald, the toy stuffed lions.[1]

She enjoyed the Godivas after dinner and before bedtime. When I stayed over with her, bringing out the box was a nightly ritual. She had sampled all the Godiva chocolates, and had her favorites. One was called "open oyster" – a milk chocolate shell filled with hazelnut praline.

ARI: Were there other foods she particularly enjoyed?

MARY ANN: The only fruit I ever saw her eat was Italian prunes. She called them "manageable" – they were small, easy to hold, had a firm texture. She enjoyed certain Russian food – especially borscht and beef Stroganoff. She made, or had Eloise make, her recipe for the Stroganoff. One of her favorite restaurants was

---

[1] Oscar and Oswald were toy lion cubs that became like family members to the O'Connors.

the Russian Tea Room on 57th Street, where she enjoyed the borscht and appetizers called pierogies. Eloise also made Ayn's recipe for Russian nut cake. That was a household favorite.

CHARLES: She liked miniature Danish pastries served with the coffee. Incidentally, she always took her coffee black, diluted with cool water. But when coffee was served to guests, it was always accompanied by heavy cream.

She also liked Asian food. When she came to Washington, she enjoyed going to Trader Vic's. And at the Sheraton Boston, where she sometimes stayed when in town for the Ford Hall Forum, she enjoyed the Polynesian-type restaurant. She was also fond of the small, dollar-size pancakes that were served at a restaurant in the Watergate Hotel in D.C. She also liked eggs Benedict, and often ordered it when she was out for a business lunch.

MARY ANN: Even though she watched her weight, she usually had dessert. One New York restaurant served an ice cream sundae that was topped off with a mound of spun sugar; it looked like spun gold; she loved its sparkling quality. Another restaurant, La Maison Japonaise, served a hot fudge sundae in a large goblet, and she recommended we all have some after dinner. At Trader Vic's, she enjoyed the ice cream ball rolled in coconut and served with chocolate sauce.

ARI: Anything she didn't like?

MARY ANN: Salads – lettuce, tomatoes, and so forth. Whenever Eloise prepared dinner, there was never a salad at Ayn's place. She once referred to salads as "grass" – which I've since learned is a Russian way of viewing salad.

ARI: Alcohol?

MARY ANN: She didn't drink; she didn't like the effects of alcohol. But she didn't frown on others drinking socially. Whenever there was a New Year's celebration at her home, Frank put out bottles of liquor – whisky, vodka, etc. – for those who wanted it. And there was always champagne at midnight. She took a sip for the occasion, that's all.

ARI: Let's turn to clothing.

MARY ANN: Her favorites were her outfits designed by Adrian, which she had purchased in Hollywood. They were classic designs, and she carried them well in spite of being rather short. She loved the feminine, dramatic look Adrian created. I've mentioned the navy blue outfit worn with the polka dot blouse. There was also a beige wool suit with a straight, slim skirt and a belted jacket with pockets. It made her look taller, and it was slenderizing. She had a floor-length, black dinner dress; its simple lines and long sleeves gave it an austere look which was relieved by a white collar. It had a nunlike quality – she called it her "Mother Superior" dress. She also had a stunning evening dress with a long sleeve on one arm only, leaving the other arm naked. She loved capes, too, and had one in black velvet.

She didn't like shapeless garments, like shifts – loose dresses without waistlines. We had a discussion about them once, and she knew exactly why she didn't like them.

ARI: What did she say?

MARY ANN: That they were too unstructured and didn't flatter the body; they looked like something you would put on if you were marooned on a desert island and desperate for something to wear – as if no thought had been given to them. That's how she characterized them.

ARI: What about casual clothes, like slacks?

MARY ANN: I've seen pictures of her from the Hollywood days where she is wearing slacks. She was thinner then. When I knew her, she had stopped wearing them. She thought a woman had to be slender to look decent in slacks.

ARI: What type of shoes did she wear?

MARY ANN: Ayn had beautiful legs. She knew it, and showed them off in high heels and sheer stockings. She especially liked platform shoes because they added to her height. There was a store on 57th Street she frequented because they had a good selection of platforms when no one else did. In the seventies, when high platforms with thick, high heels were in style again, she was delighted and bought a pair. But they were clunky and difficult to walk in; she sprained her ankle and had to stop wearing them, much to her disappointment.

CHARLES: If I may, I'd like to interject here with an anecdote about her legs. A group of her friends met at the O'Connors' apartment one evening to watch an interview show she had taped earlier. When it was over, she asked us for our reactions. I don't remember the specific comments, but everyone was complimentary about her performance. When we finished with our remarks, she asked if that was all. We were, to a person, perplexed. What else was there to say? She then said that she was disappointed that no one had a comment about how good her legs looked! It's not that none of us noticed them – I certainly did. I think we all thought her focus on the show was strictly intellectual. As it turned out, someone at the TV studio had commented on her good-looking legs, much to her pleasure.

ARI: What about colors?

MARY ANN: Her top favorite was blue-green in all shades, from muted to bright. She didn't just *like* that color, she *loved* it. But then Ayn was always enthusiastic about her favorites – she was a woman who valued her values. Frank made a point of putting touches of blue-green around the apartment – vases, ashtrays, a cigarette box, a pillow, small sculptures. And one winter she had a housecoat made in bright, blue-green corduroy. Frank found the material for her.

CHARLES: On one of her visits to D.C., she stayed at the 16th Street Hilton, where my dad had a jewelry store off the lobby. Ayn was surveying a case with costume jewelry and spotted a ring set with a large, blue-green stone, a chunky mineral of some kind. She was pleased with her find, and she bought it. The next time we saw her in New York, she was wearing a short cotton housecoat, like a model's coat, in blue-green, and the ring. She held up her hand, proudly, so we could see the souvenir from Washington. Ayn had a large collection of costume jewelry, with many blue-green pieces. Also scarves and handkerchiefs that featured her favorite color.

MARY ANN: She also wore basic colors – black and navy blue. But she didn't like what she called dirty colors – rusts, dull oranges, mustards. Her color preference extended to flowers, too. She was partial to blue hyacinth.

She had a dressing table with a large mirror. The mirror's frame was of aquamarine blue glass, and on two sides of it were little shelves. She had crystal and blue perfume bottles on the shelves, and on the table. She sat on a small, round ottoman covered in blue-green velvet.

ARI: Makeup and hair style?

MARY ANN: She didn't wear much makeup, just powder and lipstick. She looked good in bright, red lipstick and stayed away from pale pinks, which she knew made her look sallow. One time, I was wearing a lipstick that was pure orange; she found it attractive because it was unusual, a bit on the unnatural side. She wondered if she could wear it and asked me to bring her a tube. It looked good on her, but was not as flattering as her brighter, red shades.

She never changed her hairstyle – it was always the short, straight bob. It was a good style for her, because she had strong features. She said once that she would look ridiculous in curls.

When she started to appear on television, she lightened her hair color. After a haircut one day, the hairdresser put several lamps around Ayn's head to dry her hair in place. The lamps had a reddish glow, and Ayn commented that she liked the look it gave to her hair. She was surprised and pleased to learn that it could be duplicated by lightening her hair a few shades, and she had it done. Thereafter, she maintained it.

ARI: Did she visit the hairdresser regularly?

MARY ANN: No. One thing she liked about the short bob was that it was easy to maintain. At one time there was a barber who came to the house to cut both Ayn's and Frank's hair. But she did go for cuts and color, especially when she had a television appearance or other public speaking engagement.

ARI: Perfumes, scents on her dressing table?

MARY ANN: Most of the bottles were empty; they were there for decoration. There was only one scent I recall her using. How

I learned about it is interesting. I was on my way to Europe, coming from Maryland, and didn't have time to visit with her before the flight out of New York. Before I left for the airport, I had a message to call her. I couldn't imagine what she wanted to talk about.

ARI: What was it?

MARY ANN: She asked me to bring back two items for her. One was a bottle of cologne, which she couldn't find in New York. It was a hyacinth fragrance, by Floris. I found it at Harrods in London, and the sales clerk gave me the name of a store in Manhattan that carried it, which greatly pleased Ayn.

ARI: And the other item?

MARY ANN: Why, one of her favorite mountains. She wanted a postcard of Mont Blanc. She loved the serene majesty, the grandeur of it.

ARI: Speaking of mountains, she had a mineral collection, didn't she?

CHARLES: Yes, she liked blue-green stones, of course, and stones with unusual colors, or with shining crystals. Once, on a trip she was making to Washington by car, traffic was held up due to an accident. While they waited, she got out of the car and looked for interesting stones in the pavement. She saw one she liked and tried to pry it out with a key! When she told this story, she expressed her disappointment at having to leave the stone behind. However, in later years, I don't think she was actively collecting minerals any longer.

ARI: Let's turn to entertainment. Any movies she especially liked?

MARY ANN: *Casablanca*. She thought it was well-plotted, without one word of unnecessary dialogue. She liked the last scene, when the camera pulls back and up to show Rick and Louis walking across the airfield into the night, into their future.

ARI: She didn't think that Rick and Ilsa should have stayed together?

MARY ANN: No, she said that would have been bad writing, turning a suspenseful drama into a trite love story of the boy-meets-girl type. Even though the love affair between Ilsa and Rick was a major element in the plot, the movie was focused on the character of Rick and his redemption. When we meet him, he is a hard-drinking, somewhat cynical, embittered man. "I stick my neck out for no one," he says. As the story unfolds, we learn the cause of his bitterness and why he has given up. And we see him change back to the resolute man, ready to fight for freedom again. Ilsa tells him, "You have to think for both of us," and he does; he takes over, creating the movie's climax and its resolution. Incidentally, this was one of the topics we discussed during those early morning chats when I was typing *Atlas*.

Other movies she liked were these:

– Fritz Lang's *Siegfried*, a silent film, and her top favorite. When she recommended it, she remarked on how beautifully each scene was composed. She said that each frame looked like a painting.

– *Gambit*, with Shirley MacLaine and Michael Caine. She thought it was a charming romance, with an inventive plot.

This is not a complete list of her favorites. They're just the ones I remember her talking about.

ARI: Television shows?

CHARLES: The original *Perry Mason* was her favorite. She watched all the reruns of it, too. Mason's character, played by Raymond Burr, stressed intelligence and self-confidence, a man who enjoyed problem-solving. She praised the show when she wrote about it and compared it to the new *Perry Mason* show, which she panned.[2] And *The Untouchables*. She admired its hero, Eliot Ness, played by Robert Stack. His character projected the quiet intensity of a man dedicated to justice. The show also portrayed the miserable psychology of the gangsters. She wrote about this, too.[3]

---

[2] See "Perry Mason Finally Loses," *The Ayn Rand Letter*, Vol. II, No. 22, July 1973.

[3] See "The New Enemies of 'The Untouchables,'" *The Objectivist Newsletter*, Vol. I, No. 8, August 1962.

MARY ANN: *Charlie's Angels.* She enjoyed it for its Romanticism – the adventures of three intelligent, courageous, spirited heroines. She favored Farrah Fawcett. At the time, she thought that Fawcett was a possible candidate for Dagny, if *Atlas* were made into a movie.

She also enjoyed *Dragnet* for its detective, Joe Friday, played by Jack Webb. She liked his no-nonsense attitude toward crime-solving, expressed by his line, "Just give me the facts, m'am." And *Kojak*, the detective played by Telly Savalas, who was colorful in personal style, and thoughtful and direct in manner. Charles recommended *Kojak* to her.

CHARLES: If you think about these shows, you see that an element they all have in common is *human intelligence.*

ARI: What about her preferences in music?

CHARLES: She loved, more than any other music, what she called her "tiddlywink" music – those lighthearted, irresistibly gay melodies, many from the pre–World War I period. She loved operetta, too, especially Emmerich Kálmán and Franz Lehar. She had a recording of something we all called "the laughing song,"[4] which we never tired of hearing. The singers start to laugh as they are singing; their laughter is so contagious that long before the song is over everyone is laughing along with them. In classical music, she preferred Rachmaninoff, especially his *Second Piano Concerto.* And Chopin. She loved his "Butterfly" Etude. It has a "tiddlywink" quality. The O'Connors owned records of their favorites, and played them often.

MARY ANN: Besides the "tiddlywink" pieces, the ones I remember her playing most often and commenting on are:

– The love music from Moussorgsky's *Boris Godunov.* It is majestic, solemn, exalted, triumphant. It was her choice of music for Halley's theme.[5]

– The March from *The Love for Three Oranges* by Prokoviev. When it was being played, she would swing an arm in time to

---

[4] The "laughing song" is "Mausi," from *Victoria und ihr Husar*, an operetta by Paul Abraham.

[5] Richard Halley is a composer in *Atlas Shrugged.*

the music, as if she were conducting.

— *Simple Confession* [aka *Simple Aveu*] by François Thomé. She said that when she finished *Atlas*, it was what she wanted to hear. It expressed her inner state of complete serenity.

CHARLES: And we shouldn't leave out "Lensky's theme" from *Eugene Onegin* by Tchaikovsky. She loved that, too.

Chapter VIII

Gifts and Mementos

Charles and Mary Ann Sures at Their Wedding
1965

MARY ANN

ARI: Mary Ann, we know from her hand-edited, practice inscriptions in the Ayn Rand Archives, that Miss Rand gave a great deal of thought to the inscriptions she wrote in books she gave to people. Can you tell us about the inscriptions in the books you received from her?

MARY ANN: I'll do them in the order she gave them to me. The first one is *The Fountainhead:* "To Mary Ann Rukavina – Thank you for a magnificent performance and for the inspiring way you made use of the philosophy of this book – Ayn Rand, May 24, 1955."

ARI: What was the performance?

MARY ANN: A lecture I gave to my medieval art class. Ayn attended. The lecture compared a modern suspension bridge to a nonobjective painting. I asked: what made each possible, and then answered the question by explaining the underlying philosophy of each. To connect it to the course, I quoted from Roger Bacon, specifically his predictions about technology in a future civilization. To introduce philosophy, I quoted from Roark's speech[1] – the paragraph that begins "Man cannot survive except through his mind." And brought in concepts of identity and causality.

Ayn loved the lecture. She said it was the first time, to her

---

[1] Howard Roark is the hero in *The Fountainhead.*

knowledge, that *The Fountainhead* had been used in a college class. The next time I saw her, she gave me the inscribed copy of *The Fountainhead*. And a small gold pin in the shape of the dollar sign, inscribed "A is A."

ARI: Let's go to the next autograph.

MARY ANN: That was *Atlas Shrugged:* "To Mary Ann – expecting you to fight for Richard Halley as I fought for Hank Rearden.[2] Ayn, August 15, 1957."

ARI: Any memories connected with that inscription?

MARY ANN: Yes, two. One is the night we were given *Atlas*. She handed the books out, one by one. And of course everyone read his inscription immediately and thanked her. Everyone felt the same thing: what a pleasure to see *Atlas* as a *real book*! To hold it as a physical object! Then, we all sat down and started to read, ignoring her completely. This went on for a few minutes, and then Nathan started to laugh and called it to our attention.

ARI: Was she at all offended?

MARY ANN: Just the opposite. She said it was a great compliment to an author, especially since we had all read *Atlas* in manuscript. She was very pleased, and amused.

ARI: What is the other memory?

MARY ANN: A conversation Ayn and I had a few weeks later, about my inscription. I raised the subject of how one fights for Richard Halley. And we discussed the forms the battle would take – such as teaching and writing. She added that it also included every conversation I might have in which I explained the purpose and meaning of art. And then she said something that was then and has always been very important to me.

ARI: What was that?

MARY ANN: She reminded me that her goal was to write fiction, to create the kind of characters she admired and wanted to see in real life, and that all her work as a philosopher was for that purpose. She stressed the importance of pursuing values in the way one finds most interesting and gives one the most pleasure – as she had done. She said that over the years she had been

---

[2] Hank Rearden is an industrialist in *Atlas Shrugged*.

criticized for not writing her ideas in nonfiction form; some people said it was her duty to do so. She said she would never have given up fiction to write philosophical treatises, that doing so would have been self-sacrificial. In that conversation she stressed the importance of pursuing personal values, and not undertaking any battle as a duty.

ARI: And the next inscription?

MARY ANN: *We the Living*: "To Mary Ann – with my thanks for being a 'morale-building' 'assistant – Ayn, December 24, 1958." She gave all of us copies on Christmas Eve, which was close to the official publication date in 1959.

ARI: She was referring to your assistance on *Atlas Shrugged*?

MARY ANN: Yes, but also to other work I had done. After the publication of *Atlas*, I continued to do small typing jobs for her, from time to time. One of them was typing the Foreword to *We the Living*, and there's an amusing story connected with that. But first, if you look at the inscription, you see that she enclosed "morale-building" with quotation marks, and started to put quotation marks around "assistant." She apologized for the mistake, and I assured her that it was all right, that as her assistant I would correct it. Of course, I never did. It's one of my favorite inscriptions.

ARI: What were you doing to boost her morale?

MARY ANN: She knew she could count on me to come on time, get right to work, finish assignments, and so forth, in a professional manner. And I loved working for her, I always went in a buoyant mood. She said that lifted her spirits.

ARI: Tell me about the Foreword incident.

MARY ANN: I typed it from the handwritten manuscript, and then I proofread it before giving it to her. She noticed immediately a mistake I had made: I didn't type "foreword," I typed "forward." She was amused by the mistake, and said it was a good Freudian slip, that it meant I was thinking ahead, looking to the future.

ARI: Any other memories of that evening?

MARY ANN: Yes, one lovely one. And that was the Christmas tree Frank put up for Leonard. Leonard loved everything about the Christmas season, and asked for a tree. So, that year, Frank bought a small, perfectly shaped pine, some ornaments, tinsel, lights – the works. And he made a splendid tree. He placed it on a table in a dimly lit corner of the living room, and the tree twinkled and glistened in the semi-darkness. It was a cheerful sight. That, incidentally, was vintage Frank O'Connor – to create something beautiful for a friend he loved.

ARI: Are there other inscriptions?

MARY ANN: There are two more, both related to my marriage to Charles. Ayn's engagement gift to me was a cookbook: Rombauer and Becker, *Joy of Cooking*. The inscription reads, "To Mary Ann – to make it a joy, think of a certain scene in Chapter II, Part III of 'Atlas Shrugged' – with all my best wishes and love, Ayn 10/10/64."

ARI: And what is that scene?

MARY ANN: Dagny cooking breakfast for Galt in the valley. Ayn asked me to promise her that I would use it, even though she autographed it. I did use it, but first I put Saran Wrap over the autographed page to protect it. Soon, the book began to look like a cookbook in use, pages all splattered with food. It must be the only cookbook autographed by Ayn Rand! I love the inscription. It says so much about her.

ARI: What is that?

MARY ANN: Her focus on values, on making something that could be boring, like cooking, into a romantic episode. It was Ayn's reminder that a wife can find enjoyment in cooking, if it's for someone she loves. And Ayn's sense of drama, too – the philosopher giving something simple, like a cookbook, but with an inscription referring to a scene in her grand opus. It also reflects her tiddlywink, cheerful aspect.

So does the next inscription, five years later, in the copy she gave me of *Night of January 16th*: "To Mary Ann – Happy Wedding Anniversary! – Affectionately, Ayn, 1969 ('The exact date is on the book jacket.')."

ARI: You were married on January 16?

MARY ANN: Yes. Actually, it was Ayn's idea. Charles and I were thinking of getting married early in January, and sailing on a honeymoon cruise on January 17. When Ayn learned this, she suggested we get married the night before, on January 16. "It's good writing," she said.

ARI: Were you married in New York?

MARY ANN: Yes. We had a lovely wedding given by Joan and Allan Blumenthal in their apartment. Incidentally, Frank gave me away and made my bouquet – a stunning arrangement of white calla lilies. So, four years later, to celebrate our anniversary we decided to give each other copies of *Night of January 16th*, and I asked Ayn's secretary to get copies for us and deliver them to Ayn for autographs. She liked the idea and insisted on giving them to us as her gifts.

ARI: Do you have any other mementos of your friendship?

MARY ANN: I have a few. One is a note she wrote to me. We had planned to meet at her apartment and go to the Roosevelt Hotel for dinner and a lecture. When I arrived at the apartment building, the doorman handed me this note from Ayn:

"Dear Mary Ann: Please excuse me. But I had to go out and could not reach you (phoned several times, but you weren't home). I will not have time to come back home, so I'll go straight to the Roosevelt Coffee Shop. See you there – and will explain. Love, A." It's dated February 1, 1960.

When we did meet, she explained that she had been called to an unexpected business meeting with her agent. This note is an example of how scrupulous she was in her dealings with people.

ARI: In what way?

MARY ANN: Her doorman knew me, and she could easily have asked him to tell me she had to leave and would meet me in the coffee shop. In a real emergency, she would have. But, by writing the note, she let me know that it wasn't an emergency. She took the time to call me more than once and to write a note confirming our arrangements, saying she would explain. She didn't leave me to worry and wonder.

The other souvenirs are some notes and costume jewelry. There is a darling note from 1962, after I had stayed with Frisco while they were away. "With love and thanks – from Frisco" followed by Ayn's drawing of a paw print.

ARI: What was the occasion for the gift of jewelry?

MARY ANN: Her expression of thanks for the times I had come to stay with Frank while she was hospitalized. There are three pieces, two that she knew I especially liked. One is a necklace in the shape of a snake, made of silver, and green-blue glass and enamel. It always made me think of Cleopatra's asp. Another is a six-pointed star-shaped brooch, made of pieces of mother-of-pearl, with diamond chips at the star's points. Something to be worn, she said, by an elegant and feminine sheriff. And the last is a necklace I had never seen her wear, but which she thought I would like. It's a series of moonstones suspended from a delicate silver chain. She advised me to wear it against a bare neck, not on clothing, for the best effect.

When she gave them to me, she told me not to put them away as souvenirs, but to wear and enjoy them.

CHARLES

ARI: Charles, what books did Miss Rand inscribe for you?

CHARLES: I have two inscribed books. My copy of *Night of January 16th* reads, "To Charles – Happy Fourth Anniversary! – Affectionately, Ayn, 1969."

The other one is *Atlas Shrugged.* "To Charles – with my congratulations on the happiness you have achieved, and my best wishes for a future of ever-growing achievement – Affectionately, Ayn, 11/15/65."

ARI: Does the date commemorate any event?

CHARLES: The event was a conversation I had with Ayn about how Objectivism had affected my life.

ARI: And how had it?

CHARLES: In essence, it taught me that seeking happiness was morally right and the purpose of living. My reason for having the conversation was to thank her for Objectivism and tell her how it had enriched my life. And, most important, Objectivism brought Mary Ann and me together, and that is and always will be the source of the greatest happiness for both of us. Not long after the conversation, Ayn gave me the inscribed copy of *Atlas.*

ARI: Did she explain the reason for the inscription?

CHARLES: She didn't have to. One of the points she stressed in that conversation was that happiness *can* be achieved. It was up to each of us to decide what we wanted of life, to think about what values to pursue and what goals to reach – in effect, to think about what would make us happy. There are *causes* for the state of happiness which we can enact. And to reach that state is an achievement. That's the focus of the inscription, and that's why I treasure it.

ARI: Do you have other souvenirs?

CHARLES: I have a great many from the stamp collecting days with Ayn. I should say stamp collecting *years* – we started in 1971 and continued until her death in 1982. Sharing this hobby was one of the most enjoyable aspects of our friendship.

Earlier, I spoke about collecting her favorite stamps that were illustrated in her article "Why I Like Stamp Collecting." I mounted the actual stamps over the illustrations and showed her the results of my work. And, of course, I thanked her for inspiring me to revive my interest in stamps. She inscribed that copy of the article, "To Charles and Mary Ann – Thank you! Ayn Rand, 5/10/71."

ARI: What are the other stamp souvenirs?

CHARLES: Correspondence about stamps, including a number of thank-you notes from Ayn for stamps I had sent to her. I have lists of stamps she needed for her collection. And many glassine envelopes she labeled which contained stamps she sent to me – stamps she couldn't use for one reason or another. And accountings. One of my favorites is a scrap of paper with a brief, handwritten accounting she sent regarding some stamps she took from an album in that worldwide collection I talked about. It reads, "Total: I have taken 39 stamps – at 2¢ per stamp = 78¢ AR."

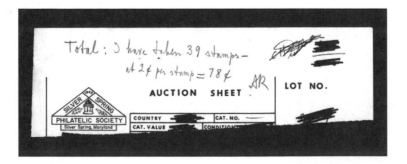

ARI: Do you have any souvenirs relating to Frank O'Connor?

CHARLES: Yes, indeed. We have four of his paintings, all still lifes. One of them is the very first still life he did in oil. It shows a crystal decanter with green liqueur, and a silver candelabrum, and a copper tray, some fruit – all lit by sunlight. Frank never gave it a title, but Ayn always called it "Benevolent Universe." We also have the candelabrum, which was one of a pair; we have both.

Another painting is the *Still Life with Apples,* a simple composition with three red apples and a small, blue ceramic vase. We have that vase, also. Mary Ann often fills it with perky daisies.

The other still lifes are studies in light and texture. One, which is unfinished, includes some artist's materials – a tube of paint, a bottle of oil, a package of cigarettes. The other still life includes a brick-colored container full of art brushes casting prominent and sharp shadows on an adjacent wall, some books (one of which is blue-green and looks like it could be *Atlas Shrugged*), a newspaper – all sitting on a lustrous surface. Both paintings have sections of drapes in the background, done in Frank's unique style of rendering cloth.

ARI: He didn't give titles to these paintings?

CHARLES: No. They weren't fully finished, and he never titled a painting until it was finished to his satisfaction.

We also have the toy drum and the artist's wooden anatomical model Frank used in *Diminishing Returns.*

ARI: How about photographs of the Sures with the O'Connors?

CHARLES: Very few of those, just the ones from our wedding album. Ayn always discouraged snapshots, so I seldom carried a camera with me on our trips to New York. But for our wedding, there were no restrictions. We didn't have a professional photographer, but many guests there had cameras. Ayn wanted a picture of the four of us, and she and Frank posed with us for that memorable occasion. We all look so happy together. It's the best souvenir of the wonderful friendship we had with Ayn and Frank.

Frank O'Connor, Ayn Rand, Charles and Mary Ann Sures
at the Sures' Wedding
1965

About the Authors

Mary Ann Sures (neé Rukavina) is an art historian, with a B.A. in history from Wayne State University and an M.A. in art history from Hunter College. She taught art history at New York University (Washington Square College) and at Hunter College. She lectures on the application of Objectivist esthetics to the visual arts. Her friendship with Ayn Rand and Frank O'Connor began in 1954. The Sures were married in 1965.

Charles Sures practiced law for 44 years, prior to his retirement in 1992. He received LL.B and LL.M degrees from George Washington University. During World War II, he served in the South Pacific as a landing craft officer in the Navy [Lt. (j.g.)]. He was a pianist, stamp collector, and aerobatic pilot. His friendship with the O'Connors began in the early 1960s. Mr. Sures died in December 2000.

The Ayn Rand Institute

The purpose of the Ayn Rand Institute (ARI) is to increase awareness of the existence and content of Ayn Rand's philosophy, Objectivism. Institute programs include:

1. The Objectivist Academic Center, which offers graduate and undergraduate courses on the content and methodology of Objectivism.

2. High school essay contests based on Ayn Rand's novels *Anthem* and *The Fountainhead*.

3. The Ayn Rand Archives.

4. Essay contests for university students, based on Ayn Rand's novel *Atlas Shrugged*.

5. A campus speakers bureau and other support for college Objectivist clubs, such as the "Student Survival Guide" on the Institute's Web site.

6. Newspaper editorials applying Objectivism to current events.

7. ARI's Self-Defense Kit for Capitalists and other programs that provide a moral defense for business and free markets.

For information on these and other programs, visit the Ayn Rand Institute Web site at www.aynrand.org.